NĀGĀNANDAM

BY

HARSHAVARDHANA

SRI GARIB DASS ORIENTAL SERIES NO—59

NĀGĀNANDAM
by
HARSHAVARDHANA

Translated into English by

LEELA DEVI

SRI SATGURU PUBLICATIONS
DELHI—INDIA

Published by
SRI SATGURU PUBLICATIONS

A division of
INDIAN BOOKS CENTRE
Oriental Publishers
40/5, Shakti Nagar
DELHI - 110007
(INDIA)

I.S.B.N.—81-7030-121-1
First Edition :—DELHI—1988

Printed in India
Composed by AMAR PRINTERS
1332/90, Tri Nagar, Delhi-35.
Printed by Kiran Mudran
Mayapuri, Delhi.

Contents

INTRODUCTION	vii-xvi
FIRST ACT	1-13
SECOND ACT	14-28
THIRD ACT	29-41
FOURTH ACT	42-55
FIFTH ACT	56-75

Introduction

HARSHAVARDHANA (606-647 A.D.)

Our knowledge of Harsha of Kanauj is full and precise because of Bana's 'Harshacharita' and Hiuen Tsan'g 'Travel'. "His personal characteristics and the details of his administ ration, as recorded by men who knew him intimately, enable us to realize him as a living person who achieved greatness by his capacity and energy". (V. Smith). 'Harshacharita' is not a garbled and over-coloured narrative of an admiring poet. It is a mine of social and political information. "It is as much based on real events as Scot's 'Quentin Durward' or 'Waverley'. Of the Chinese traveller, Hiuen Tsang, T. Watters observes : "He had a rare combination of moral and intellectual qualities and traits common to Chinest set off by a marked individuality". His 'Travels' is noted for remarkable descriptive power, keenness of observation and accuracy of record.

Born in 590 A.D. Harsha was the son of Prabhakaravardhana and Yasomati. Prabhakaravardhana was the ruler of Thanesar from 583 to 605 A.D. a scion of the Guptas and a descendant of a pious Saiva, Pushpabhuti, the founder of the family. He assumed the title of 'Maharajadhiraja' and 'Paramabhattaraka', 'Lion to the Hun Deer,' and 'the Destroyer of Gujerat, Gandhara' and Malwa'. When he died, his eldest son Rajyavardhana ascended the throne. Soon the new king had a trial of regal felicity, for the Malwa king and Sasanka of Bengal encompassed the death of Grahavarman Maukhari, the husband of his sister, Rajyasri. He led a punitive expedition and routed the aggressors ; but he was killed by Sasanka. Harsha, his younger brother, was just sixteen years of age. Bana and Hieun Tsang attest that he was at first unwilling to accept the crown. C.V. Vaidya, on the other hand, says that his refusal was only with regard to the throne of Kanauj. Any how at the instance of Bodhisattva Avalokitesvara he became king (606). He commemorated his accession by founding a new era known as the Harsha era (606).

His first task was to avenge his enemies and to rescue his sister who had fled to the Vindhya forests. He discovered and saved her from self-immolation ('anumarana'). Within six years he destroyed his foes and securly established himself on the throne.

The elephants were not unharnassed, nor the soldiers unhelmeted" until he attained his defeat at the hands of Pulakesin II. Though truthful and high-minded he does not mention this unhappy incident because it was not customary to record mllitary reverses. Contradictory descriptions are extant about this clash between the northern and the southern lords. Hiuen Tsang writes that Harsha failed to effect the conquest of Maharashtra in spite of the aid of a myriad army of the five rivers of the Indus. The victorious Pulakesin assumed the title of Paramesvara. The Aihole inscription attests to this well-earned victory. The date of the battle is variously given : Smith, 620 ; R.K. Mookherji, 612 and R.S. Tripathi, 630.

In 635 Harsha defeated the ruler of Valabhai, Dhruvasena II, to whom he gave his daughter in marriage. In 643 he conducted a campaign against Kongod (Ganjam Dt.) Meanwhile, two years before, he sent an embassy to China. His empire was now more than that held by the Guptas, from the Brahmaputra to Kathiawar without Rajaputana, Sind and major portion of the Punjab.

His religion :—His religion underwent varied evolution. In his early life he was the rising hope of the stern unbending Saivaites. Later he showed Buddhist leanings as evidenced by Bana. Hiuen Tsang calls him a Buddhist from the outset who had the name of Siladitya. An ardent Hinayanist, Harsha was converted by him to Mahayanism. According to the Chinese traveller he strictly forbade animal sacrifice erected stupas, rest houses and monasteries, summoned frequent synods and enforced the Buddhistic ideals. Though not a passionate thinker and dialectician, he was a great propagandist. In the Kanauj conference, 643, which was attended by several thousands of scholars the Chinese Master of the Laws wos honoured by him. Hiuen Tsang gave an eloquent exposition of Mahayanism and challenged his opponents with his head as a wager. In the Allahabad quinquennial gathering Harsha distributed all his savings as gifts.

His administration :—Harsha's administration was one man's rule. He concentrated in himself all the threads of government. By his vigilance, foresight, justness and nobility he carried on the duties of kingship benevolently. He toured his empire often and posted himself with first-hand knowledge. One-fourth of the revenue of the state he used for maintaining the government and state worship. One-sixth of the produce of the land was the land imposition. The Mauryan methods of enquiry into civil and sriminal cases were continued ; trial by ordeal was the common Of the usual 'chaturanga' of the army, the charit unit was absent under Harsha, and honoured place was given to the elephant corps. Trade and commerce were regularised and guild organisation existed. The people were honest and highly moral. The untouchables were segregated and sati was practised. The government attached great importance to the preservation of official records. Besides the sylavan abodes of learning two universities were far-famed. These were in Valabhi and Nalanda and were modelled like the modern universities with official hierarchy, (for example Vice-Chancellor Dharmapala of Kanchi). Many temples and buildings were built with several storeys and the statues of the Buddha.

His literary contribution : Harsha is credited with the authorship of three works. Ratnavali, Nagananda and Priyadarsika. I-tsino says that he prepared Jatakamala or the birth-stories of the Buddha. Harsha is also made the author of several poems and grammatical works. His contemporaries whom he patronised were Bana, the author of Kadambari, Mayura, the brother-in-law of Bana, the author of Kamasastra and Suryasataka, Matanga Divakara, and Bhartrihari, the poet philosopher grammarian. He died in 640 A.D.

Harsha easily takes his rank among the great Hindu kings of India, Lacking the warmth and passion of Asoka, the versatility and valour of Samudragupta and the zeal and electicism of Kanishka he excelled them all by his unbeuding idealism.' Hc is often compared to Marcus Aurelius with whom ae had much in common, but he was not, like the croward philosopher of ancient Rome "something melancholy, circumscribed and inffectual". At once a soldier, scholar, poet and statesman he closed one epoch.

The glorious heritage of Hindu India was slowly being gathered into the aeon of the Past. Harsha was the last great Hindu King.

Identity of Harsha

The prologue of the play Nagananda mentions the name of Sri Harsha as its author. But there flourished in the ancient literary world of this country three persons of the same name Sri Harsha, king of Kashmir, Sri Harsha, the author of the 'Naishadha Kavya', and Sri Harsha, familiarly known as Harshavardhana, kinq of Kanauj, Tradition, historical facts and literary collation establish that it was the ruler of Kanauj, not his two other namesakes, that wrote the Nagannanda.

Vincent Smith characterises Harsha of Kashmir as "a half-insane tyrant" "justly described as the Nero of Kashmir" and places him in the latter part of the eleventh century. Prof. Wilson (Selected specimens of the Theatre of the Hindus) assigns to him the years of kingship between 1113 and 1125 A.D. Dhananjaya's 'Dasarupa', a work on Dramaturgy, written at the close of the tenth century, contains many references to the Nagananda. The ruler of Kashmir, therefore, even though he had the name of Harsha could not have been the author of this drama. Further history and common belief ascribe to his short regime nothing but double-dyed iniquity and tyranny, and Kalhana in his 'Rajatarangini', "the nearest approach to a work of regular history in extant Sanskrit literature," does not ally him with any literary production.

The author of the 'Naishandha Kavya, Sri Harsha, could not have also been the author of the 'Nagananda', for the writer of the latter was, and the former was not a monarch controlling several feudatory chieftains. In the Prologue of the drama the Manager says :

(Lotus-like feet of King Sri Harshadeva'; 'our lord ; 'that same monarch who gladdens the hearts of all people and with a view to oblige us'). The last verse of the 22nd conto of the Naishadha Kavya records the author's acceptance from the king of Kanyakubja a seat in the royal court in token of his superiority to other poets. Hence he was not a royal literary writer. Each canto repeats two lines wdich give the name of the father and mother of the author, Hira and Mamalladevi. The kavya refers to to all his compositions, but does not mention the Nagananda.

Further, one of his works 'Sthairyavicharana' is exclusively concerned with the repudiation of the Buddhistic doctrines and he himself could not have extolled the deeds of the Bodhisathva and high Buddhistic tenets in another of his work, the Nagananda. Moreoverhe is supposed to have lived in the 12th century, and the Nagananda was written five centuries before. Thus by the process of elimination we conclude that Harshavardhana of Kanauj wrote the drama and that he was also the author of two other works, the Ratnavali and the Priyadarsika. An examination of the style, construction, arrangement of the Act and the recurrence of sentiment and thought in the three works support the theory of common authorship.

The Source of The Nagananda and Deviatiods From the Original

1. The Source.

In the Kaviprasamsa portion of the introduction of the play, it is stated that the plot of the drama is taken from the Vidyadharajataka. But the jataka-collections so far known to scholars do not contain the story of Jimutavahana. This has naturally led us to tnink the Vidyadharajataka, current during king Harsha's time must have been lost to us.

Brahatkatha of Gunadhya (I Century A.D.) forms another source of our play. Unfortunately the original Brahatkatha, written in Paisaci, is now lost but the two latter-day Sanskrit works containing the versified resume of the stories of the Paisaci-work are happily preserved. The two works are Somadeva's Kathasaritsagara and Ksemendra's Brhatkathamanjari. The story of Jimutavahana is found in the two Sanskrit works with slight variation. Inasmuch as the two works are based on Gunadhya's Brahatkatha, we can safely conclude that our play-wright must have drawn on the Brahatkatha for the plot of his play.

In the two Sanskrit works mentioned above, we have the story of Jimutavahana narrated twice, one short and the other long in two different contexts.

The Difference Between the short and the long Narratives

In the former, the story of the former birth of Jimutavahana, Malayavati and Mitravasu is found fully narrated, while it has but a meagre reference in the latter. The first meeting of the hero and the heroine isnot mentioned in the shorter version while their courtship is described in full in the other. Sankacuda, the serpent-chief the one is, that informs the hero of the agreement between Vasuki and Garuda, in the former while Mitravasu does it in the latter. Again, in the short narrative, Jimutavahana manages to send Mitravasu away from the sea shore on some pretext, while in the longer one, Mitravasu leaves the scene on being summoned by his father. In the shorter narrative mention is not made of Cudamani, the crest-jewel, while in the other it is said to have fallen at the feet Malayavati who shows it to her elders there. In the brief narrative the parents of Jimutavahana do not know of the fate befallen their dear son and so not follow the bloody trail, while in the other, the sight of the rest jewel kindles the supernatural powers in them and makes them trace out their victim-son· In the short narrative finally, the serpents that had been victimised are brought back to life and happiness by a nectarine shower, while in the long one it is done by the sheer power of the penitent Garuda himself. Lastly, the name of the hero's enemy is mentioned as Matanga in the shorter version of the Kathasaritsagara while the other one is without it. The shorter narrative is more akin to the plot of our play and has a natural setting in the original Brahatkatha.

Again some slight discrepancies exist in the respective narratives of the Kathasaritsagara and the Brahatkathamanjari.

In the Katasaritsagara it is said that Jimutavahana's confidante is one hermit boy while in the other it is said to be one Madhukara. In the Brihatkata manjari it is said that the hero converting himself with the pair of red garments throws himself on the slab of execution while it ie not mentioned in the other. The crest jewel of the hero, as he is being lascerated by the beak and talons of Garuda, falls at the lap of Malayavati, in this work, while it falls at her feet in the other.

Deviations from the original narratives and the dramatic purpose served by them.

In the original story as we have it, Jimutavahana gives away in compassion the Kalpaka tree to the miserable world ; but immediately after, takes fright at the loss of the divine tree and goes to the forest with his parents suspecting attack from his enemies.

In the Drama, the hero decides to go to the forest not out of fear for attack from his enemies but only to serve his aged parents who had retired in peace to Malaya mountain. By this the playwright brings out the filial piety of the hero, one of the chief traits of a Bodhisattva. Not only that, the hero is also made out to be a person full of daya-vira.

In the original story, the hero goes to the temple of Gauri, sees Malayavati, gets to know all about her from her maid and makes friends with her.

In the Drama, though the meeting of the hero and the heroine happens in the temple of Gauri, the hero does not know about her, not even her name, when the advent of the hermit takes the heroine off the scene. This helps for the intensity of Sringara leading to the dejection of the heroine and her attempted suicide and the hero's great concern and prompt intervention.

Malayavati, according to the original story is taken off the scene at Gauri's temple by summons from her mother.

In the Drama, it is done by the hermit-Kulapati.

In the original, the heroine attempts suicide, being unable to bear the anguish of separation, delay and fancied disappointment ; and she is prevented from the perilous and precipitous deed by Goddeas Gauri by infusing hopes into her.

In the Drama, the heroine attempts suicide on hearing that the hero has his heart on another ; and by lucky chance, the hero himself who happens to be near the scene, appears and averts the calamity. This certainly serves to heighten the Srinagara by contacting the hero and the heroine at a very critical juncture.

The Drunkard's Scene, in its entirety, is introduced only by the playwright to kindle the hasya which, in a sense, is a feeder of erotics. Not only that. The side splitting laughter produced by this humorous scene, prepares the audience for the pathos and tragic elements of the subsequent scenes.

The Matanga-incident is not found in the original, while that is introduced by the playwright in the Drama to bring out the perfect state of dispassion and ahimsa in the hero, a Bodhisattva.

In the original story, the cudamani or the crest jewel of the hero falls, as he is being lascerated by the beak of Garuda, at the feet of Malayavati, while the father comes to know of his son's fate by his power of introspection.

The playwright has made the jewel fall at the feet of the father thereby showing the great filial piety of the son.

In the original, on knowing the fate of her lord, Malayavati, at her own initiative, tries to put an end to herself.

But in the Drama, the whole family and Sankhacuda, follow the bloody trail, arrive at the bloody scene and prepare to enter fire. The family bond, Sankhacuda's character and patho all this is heightened thereby.

In the original no mention is made of the Prayascitta or atonement on the part of Garuda.

In the Drama, Garuda amply atones for his thoughtless misdeeds and sins, promises to refrain from killing the serpents and leaves the scene with a penitent heart.

In the original the slaughtered serpents are revived by the grace of the Goddess, Gauri.

In the Drama, Garuda himself flies up, releases a shower of nectar and revives the dead snakes thereby completing his act of expiation.

The above deviations apart, there are also some minor differences between the original narrative and our play. A few instances may be cited. In the original there is no mention made of the dream as a good prognostic of the prospective marriage of the heroine with the hero, while the Drama has it. The stock-in-trade, picture-drawing by the hero of the heroine is not found in the original narrative. The account of the previous birth of the hero is found in the original while it is not found in the Drama. The story of Vinata-Kadru quarrel is found in the original narrative while the Drama has not got it because it serves no dramatic purpose.

Influence of Buddhism on the Play

The play opens with the invocation of the blessings of the Buddha, the All-Conqueror, on the audience. The hero is explicitly called a Bodhisattva. The plot of the play is drawn from the Buddhistic Jataka-stories. The story revolves round the great Buddhistic moral namely, ahimsa, non-injury to animals, and suffering and sacrifice for that supreme cause. The hero has all the characteristics of the Buddhistic saint. Thus the play is predominantly Buddhistic in its setting.

Non-injury to animals—no need to say of human benigs—has been the absolute ethics, mahavrata with Vedic religton too. A Vedic Hindu can practise non-violence as his or her absolute ethics even as Harischandra practised Truth as absolute ethics and Sri Rama practised tyaga likewise. There can be no half-way house, no compromise, no equieoque with absolute ethics. Even a white lie is a lie with Harischandra. Even the killing of animals in holy sacrifice is sin from the view point of ahimsa as absolute ethics. Did not Dadhici a Vedic sage give his back-bone to Indra for the supreme world cause ? Did not Rama give away Sita for the sake of his subjects taking his sole stand on the principle absolute tyaga ? Likewise Jimutavahana sacrificed his life for the sake of the serpent. This ahimsa has been specially emphasised by Buddhism and so is the absolute ethics of a true Bodhisattva. A Hindu who is ritual-ridden, may noi appreciate this aspect of a Bodhisattva. From his point of view the play may be Buddhistic in tone. But from an absolutist's point of view this play is as much Hindu as it is Buddhistic.

The fundamental non-difference between these schools of religion has been ably effected by Harsa in this play. That is why he introduces the Hindu Goddess Gauri both at the beginning and at the end of the drama and also the Hindu bird Garuda.

Let us examine how far the principle of self-sacrifice as absolute ethics is justified. The Buddha renounced the world of plenty and mortified his flesh to evolve a perfectly blissful world, to completely annual the ills of the world. Was he able to achieve his aim ? Was he able to usher in nirvana to all ? No. In this aim the Buddha failed and his religion has to accept defeat. So long as there is this world there is bound to be suffering and the painful pairs of opposites. By taking to a virtue as absolute ethics, an individual may become perfect and uplift a community or a country at the most. History shows that the whole wolrd cannot be purified. To improve the entire world is to improve it out of existence. Jimutavahana's suffering would have ended in the ending himself up ultimately but for the timely advent of Goddess Gauri. His sacrificing his heirloom the Kalpaka-tree, his kingdom and his own life would have made him only a perfect soul, a modes for a few other souls, his followers, perhaps. But suffering cannot be permanently eradicated from the entire Universe. Suffering may lead the suffering individual only into nirvana, but mayfail to lead the entire universe into it.

In the above light we can say that the Naganunda is predominantly Buddhistic from a relative point of view. But from the point of view of absolute ethics the play has the setting in universal religion.

From the invocation to the Buddha in the Nandi and the circumstancc that the play describes the incidents of the Buddha's life in his work as Jimutavahana, it is possible to say that the play has a Buddhistic colouring ; but it may be too soon to affirm that the main purpose of it is to illustrate a Buddhistic doctrine of Universal humaneness. The rule of compassion is inculcated in all ancient Hindu ethical literature and is essentially pre-Buddhistie in its origin. Garuda is an Aryan (or rather a Hindu) God and the appearance of the Goddess Gauri and shower of nectar marking the happy culmination are Hindu in their core".

Soothradara	: Manager
Nati	: His wife.
Hero	: Jimutavahana
Vidushaka	: Atreya.
Heroine	: Malayavati.
Maids of Heroine	: Navamalika, Chaturika. Manoharika.
Tapasa	: Shandilya,
Prince of Siddhas	: Mitravasu.
Villain	: Sekharaka.
Servant of Sekharaka	: Kanchukeeya.
Pratihara	: Sunanda.
Old Woman	: Mother of Sankhachuda.
Sankhachuda	: Serpent Youth.
Garuda	: King of birds.
Jimutaketu	: Father of Jimutavahana.
Devi	: Wife of Jimutaketu.
Gauri	: Goddess.

THE NAGANANDA

Act I

NANDI

Using the pretext of meditation, of which lady are you thinking ? Opening your eyes, at least a moment, look at us who are tortured with the arrows of Kama,

You are falsely called a kind person, you do not save us, where can there be another more heartless than you ?

Being thus teased by the brides of Mara, may Jina, the all conquering Lord Buddha, protect you all.

And

"Though marked by Kama as a target of his drawn bow, and regarded by his warriors with the beat of drums,

With jubilant dance and eyed by heavely maiden with tremulous leers, parted inviting lips and attractive smiles,

He who remained steady in his meditation in the hour of his enlightenment,

Who was considered with bowed heads and thrilled bodies by Siddhas and by Indra gazed with amazement, that Lord of sages may protect you all"—

Stage Manager (*At the end of this prayer enter Stage Manager*)

The Kings who have assembled here as vassals at the lotus feet of his majesty King Harsha, at the Indra festival to-day, called me with due respect and said.

"We have heard rumours that our lord, His majesty King Harsha has written a play called Nagananda which is based on the story of Vidyadhara Jataka. We hear that this drama has an original plot. We have not seen it produced. So, with high respect for King Harsha, and consideration for us, you should stage it properly."

So, after arranging the costumes I shall proceed to fulfil their wish.

(*Walks around and looks at the audience*)

I believe the minds of the audience are full of expectation, because—

Sri Harsha is the master of his muse, This assemblage is appreciative of merit,

The stories of Bodhisattva do catch the popular fancy, And we are expert in the art of acting,

Any of these facts is enough for producing the desired effect, but how much more so,

Does this whole set of excellences when combined through my abundant good fortune !

I shall, therefore call my wife and arrange for the (preliminary) performance.

(*Turning and looking toward the retiring room*)

My lady, you are amiable to all-priests, attendants, and kinsmen alike, you are the enlivening spirit of my house as the swan is that of a lake,

You are sweet of disposition and becomest modest in the presence of strangers, as the lotus droop at the appearance of the moon. Pray, just come here. I have something on hand.

Actress (*Entering in tears*)

My lord, here I am, a wretched being.

Stage Manager (*Observing the Actress*)

My lady, when Nagananda is going to be staged here, why do you weep for nothing ?

Actress

My lord, why shouldn't I weep, when I see revered father and mother-in-law, growing indifferent to worldly affairs due to old age, have retired to the penance-grove, considering in their mind that you are fit to bear the burden of the family.

Stage Manager

What ! Have my parents retired to the forests, leaving me behind ? What am I to do now ?

(*Reflecting*)

What is proper now ? How can I deprive myself of the pleasure of serving my elders and stay here at home ? For,—

> To serve my parents, relinguish my inherited wealth,
> Resort to the forests, like Jimutavahana.

(*Exeunt both*)

End of Prelude (*Enter Jimutavahana and Vidushaka*)

Jimutavahana (*Dejectedly*)

Friend Atreya,—

> I know that youth is the season of rising passion; I am also not unaware of its transience,
>
> Who on earth does not know that it flouts all discretion between right and wrong ?
>
> Be it ever so reprehensible because of passion's sway, it can still contribute to my happiness.
>
> If I pass it in serving my parents with the same devotion as ever.

Vidushaka (*Indignantly*)

My dear friend, have you not grown sick of enduring so long the hardships of life spent in the forest for the sake of these two (wasted) old people who are more dead than alive ? Should it please you to have my advice, it is time you desisted from your resolve of attending on your parents and enjoyed the luxuries of the King's life which is so alluring on account of affording surfeit of all desires.

Jimutavahana

You are not right, my friend. For,—

> The majesty a man acquires by sitting on the ground waiting upon his parent, can it ever be his while he sits on the throne ?

> The pleasure a man finds in shampooing the feet of his parent, can it ever be his while he rules over a number of kings ?
>
> The satisfaction a man gets by partaking of what is left after feeding his parents, can it ever be his when he enjoys the lordship of the three worlds ?
>
> Even king ship, I daresay, is a curse for him who neglects his parent. What is there then to commend it ?

Vidushaka (*Aside*)

Oh ! What great delight does this service of parents give him ?

(*Reflecting*)

Well, I shall then say this.

(*Aloud*)

My friend, I did not simply mean to refer to the life of royal luxuries in my words. There are other things, too, which you have to do.

Jimutavahana

My friend, I have indeed fulfilled my duty. Look,

> The ministers have already been set on the path of rightousness. Good men are living in happiness now.
>
> Kinsmen have been raised to a status equal to mine. Order has been established in the state.
>
> Even the Kalpaka tree which yields them more than they desire, I have given to the needy.
>
> What more remains to be done after this ? Or tell me, what you have in mind.

Vidushaka

You know, my friend, the desperate dare-devil, Mantangadeva is your foe. When he is your next-door neighbour I am afraid your kingdom is insecure without you, however well-administered it may be under your Prime Minister.

Jimutavahana

Do you fear that Matanga will annex my kingdom ?

Vidushaka

Certainly.

Jimutavahana

Even if he does, what matters ? I hold everything, including my own body, as a sacred trust for the good of others. That I have not voluntarily given it (*i.e.*, my Kingdom) away is due to my reverence to my father's wishes. But why bother about a trifle like this ? Better I should carry out the behest of my father. Father has commanded me saying, "Darling ! Jimutavahana, flowers, grass and rice have been practically exhausted from this place by constant consumption Go, therefore, to the Malaya mountain and find out a place of hermitage fit for our living." So, come, let us go to Malaya Mountain.

Vidushaka

As you command. Come Sir.

Vidushaka (*Both walk about*) (*Looking ahead*)

Look, my friend, look here ! This Malaya breeze, laden heavily with fragrance from its contact with fresh and shady groves of sandal trees and wafting the cool sprays tossed by mountain rills dashing upon rugged rocks, thrills you my friend like the embrace of the sweet-heart anxiously waiting for the first meeting, and remaves the fatigue of the journey.

Jimutavahana (*Observing*)

O' we have already reached the Malaya mountain.

(*Looking all around*)

How lovely it is ! For—

> Here flows the sap of sandalwood trees broken by elephants in rut as they rub their temples against them.
>
> Here the vaults of caves are resonant with the dash of the breakers.
>
> Here the rocks of pearly white (marble) bear the red footprints of Siddha women walking on them.
>
> Malaya hills are indeed a fine resort and fill my mind with great excitement.

Come, let us climb it and find out a hermitage suitable for habitation.

(*They act as if climbing*)

Jimutavahana (*Indicating an omen*)

Friend,

My right eye throbs, I have no desire for anything. The word of the wise cannot be untrue. Then what possibly could it mean ?

Vidushaka

My dear friend, it indicates something good that is going to happen to you.

Jimutavahana

May it be as you say.

Vidushaka (*Joyfully*)

Look there, my friend, it appears to be a penancegrove. How magnificent it is with its dense and shady trees ! Thick curls of smoke laden with the fumes of fragrant oblations rise from it. The herds of animals (deer) lie in footpaths with an air of reassurance.

Jimutavahana

Friend, you have guessed well. This is surely a penance grove. for here,—

Out of compassion indeed, the bark of trees have been removed in thin strips, for garments

Old and broken waterpots are visible at the bottom of sky-clear waters of the brooks.

Broken belts of munja grass flung away by students (Brahmacharis) are seen scattered here and there.

The parrot repeats the verses of Sama hymn as it hears them everyday.

Come, let us enter and see.

(*They act as if entering*)

Jimutavahana (*Looking all round*)

How inviting is the serene charm of the penance-grove! Here the contented sages are busy discussing the doubtful passages of the Vedic texts, the students, while repeating their lessons, are cutting the fresh fire-wood and the hermit girls are filling the basins of young plants with water. What !—

Have even the trees here been taught the etiquette of receiving the guests? For, they extend to me a sweet welcome as it were, with the humming of the bees.

They make obeisance to me as it were with their boughs bending low with fruit, and they present an offering of arghya to me as it were by shedding their flowers.

This penance-grove is really a habitable place. I believe we shall have peace while living here.

Vidushaka

Friend, why is it that the deer here have slightly turned their necks ? They have stopped munching and the half chewn grass are falling from there motionless mouths. They seem to be listening to something with an ear erect and attentive and eyes closed.

Jimutavahana (*Lending an ear*)

Friend, you have rightly noticed it. For surely,——

These deer, bending their necks and ceasing to crunch the grass held between there teeth,

Listen to some song, the words of which are sweet and clear, and which, mingling with the sonorous tune of the guitar

As if with the humming of bees, displays the successive modulations of grave and acute pitches

With the various notes arising from their proper places.

Vidushaka

Friend, who could be singing in the penance-grove ?

Jimutavahana

As the strings plucked by a delicate finger do not twang very loudly and the song, too, is mainly being sung in low and sweet tones, I presume it is some celestial damsel who is singing to the accompaniment of a lute to propitate the deity in that—

(*Pointing in front with the tip of his finger*)

—temple.

Vidushaka

Come, friend, let us visit this temple.

Jimutavahana

A good idea. Gods must be worshipped.

(*Advancing and then stopping suddenly*)

But friend, there may be a lady whom it may be objectionable for us to see. So, let us move behind these tamala trees and wait for the opportunity of having a view of the deity.

(*They do so*)

(*Enter Malayavati seated on the ground and playing on the lute and her Maid*)

Malayavati (*Sings to the accompaniment of the lute*)—

Oh, Gauri who shines like the golden dust on the filament of a lotus bloom,

My heart's desire be met with your favour, Oh Goddes.

Jimutavahana (*Lending ear*)

O friend, what a voice and what an accompaniment ! For,—

Distinctness has now been attained here through the 'distinguishing' mode of playing, in all its ten forms,

The tempo, in its three-fold division of allegro, moderato, and adagio, has been clearly marked ;

All three pauses, with the "gopucha" first, have been brought out in due order ;

All the three styles of instrumental playing--tranquil, lively, and intermediate-have been appropriately, shown.

Cheti

Princess ! You have played long enough, I say. Dont your fingers ache indeed ?

Malayavati

Chaturika, my girl, how can I feel the ache, playing before the Goddess ?

Cheti (*Tuntingly*)

Princess, I mean to say what is the good of playing before this Goddess who is so heartless ? What a long time have you been trying to please her, with vows and fasts so exacting of a young maiden but I don't see if she has shown any favour to you !

Vidushaka

My friend, she is a maiden, I am sure. What objection can there be to our looking at her ?

Jimutavahana

No harm, I should think. It is no sin to look at girls who are not yet married. But I am afraid that no sooner does she see us than she may leave the place in nervousness born of bashfulness so natural to her young age. So let us see her from behind this screen of creepers.

(*Both see in that manner*)

Vidushaka (*Seeing, with amazement*)

Look, my friend, look ! Not only does she ravish the ear by skill on the lute, but she equally feasts the eye with her beauty which matches her art. I wonder who she is ? Is she a girl from heaven, or a Naga-maiden, or the daughter of a Vidyadhara or one born of a Siddha family ?

Jimutavahana (*Looking at her with longing*)

Friend, I cannot tell who she is, but this much I know that—

> If she be a damsel from heaven, then the thousand eyes of Indra are well rewarded,
>
> If she be a Naga-maiden, then it is wrong to say that Nether world has no moon, with such a face to illumine, it !
>
> If she be a Vidyadhara girl, then indeed our race stands superior to all other races ;
>
> And if she be born in a Siddha family, then the Siddhas have won immortal fame in all the three worlds.

Vidushaka (*Looking at the Hero, joyfully aside*)

Luckily at long last, he has fallen into the snare of Kama, or rather

(*Pointing to himself*)

of Brahman, namely, myself.

Cheti (*Affectionately*)

I tell you, Princess, what is the use of playing before this heartless Goddess ?

(*She snatches away the lute*)

Malayavathi (*Angrily*)

Maid, don't blaspheme the Goddess Gauri. She has already conferred a vara (blessing) on me tonight.

Cheti (*Joyfully*)

Tell me, Princess, of what nature that favour is ?

Malayavati

Dear Girl, this even now I clearly remember that while in my dream I was playing on the lute as I am doing now, the Goddess Gauri said, "My child, I am pleased with your extraordinary skill in playing on the lute and unusual devotion to me, so rare to find in one so young. So, the Emperor of the Vidyadharas shall take your hand in marriage before long."

Cheti

Princess, if that be so, then why call it a dream ? The Goddess has indeed granted you the boon of your heart.

Vidushaka (*Hearing it*)

Well, friend, now is the right time for us to see the Goddess. Come, let us enter.

Jimutavahana

No, I shall not go in.

Vidushaka (*Dragging the affectedly unwilling HERO by force and approaching*)

Lady, the maid has spoken the truth. Here is rhe love of your heart, the Goddess has promised you.

Malayavati (*Rising up in embarassment and pointing to Jimutavahana*)
Maid, who is this man ?

Cheti (*Observing Jimutavahana closely*)

From his appearance which is indeed matchless, methinks, he is the very boon granted you by the Goddess.

Jimutavahana (*Malayavati stands up and looks at Jimutavahana longingly and coyly*)

> Oh, tremulous and long eyed one with rich and full breasts heaving at everybreath, this body,
>
> Has been over strained with penance, why strain it more in agitation ?

Malayauati (*Aside, in whispers*)

Maid, I fear I am too nervous to stay in his presence.

Vidushaka (*Looking at the HERO bashfully with a side-glance, she stands with her face averted*)

Madam, is this the etiquettee of your penance-grove that a guest who happens to arrive here is not greeted even by words ?

Cheti (*Looking at the Heroine aside*)

Her eye seems to be fixed amorously at him. So, I shall speak like this.

(*Aloud*)

Princess, what the Brahmana says is correct. Hospitality towards a guest is expected of you. Why, I wonder, you should stand like undecided about your duty towards this honourable gentleman ? Or wait, I shall myself do what is proper.

(*Addressing the HERO*)

Your Honour is welcome. Pray adorn this place by taking your seat here.

Vidushaka

My friend, she has said well. Come, let us sit and refresh ourselves a while.

Jimutavahana

You are right.

(*Both sit down*)

Malayavati (*Bashfully*)

Don't you take liberties, mocking girl. If, by chance, some hermit were to see me, he would consider me to be immodest.

Tapasa (*Enter Tapasa*)

Kulapati Kausika has bid me, "Sandilya, at the instance of his father, Prince Mitravasu has gone to see today Prince Jimutavahana, the would-be Emperor of the Vidyadharas, who is putting up somewhere here on the Malaya hill, to get him as husband of Malayavati, his sister. Waiting for his return, Malayavati may miss her midday prayer, so you may go and fetch her here." Accordingly, I shall go to the temple of Gauri.

(*Walking about and looking closely at the ground*)

Whose foot-prints on the dust could these be, that clearty show the marks of an Emperor ?

(*Observing Jimutavahana in front*)

Surely, these are the steps of this noble person. For,—

> A well-marked excrescence is on his head and a lovely ring of hair is between his brows.
>
> His eyes are like lotus and his chest vies with that of Vishnu (or a lion),
>
> Both hands bear the sign of wheel. From these signs, I believe, He is a man who will not rest till he has risen to the status of a Vidyadhara soverign.

Or why donbt it ? He must be Jimutavahana,

(*Observing Malayavati*)

Our Princess is also here !

(*Looking at both*)

After a long time Fate would do the right thing if this pair which is so well-matched, are united.

(*Approaching and addressing Jimutavahana*)

Hail to you !

Jimutavahana

I, Jimutavahana, greet you, revered sir.

(*Wishes to give his seat*)

Tapasa

Don't please, don't get up. It is you who ought to be honoured by us, for a guest deserves honour, from all. So, please sit comfortably.

Jimutavahana

All right.

Malayavati

I bow to you, sir

Tapasa (*Addressing Malayavati*)

Good lady, may you be united with a husband worthy of you! Princess, preceptor Kausika has asked you to come quickly, as the time for the midday prayer is passing away.

Malayavati

As our preceptor commands.

(*To herself*)

On one side the command of the proceptor and on the other the pleasure of the sight of the beloved,

To go or not to go, on the horns of this dilemma doth my mind sway me even now.

(*Rising up she sighs, and looking at Jimutavahana with longing bashfulness, exit with Hermit and her maid*)

Jimutavahana (*Sighing and looking at Malayavati as she retreats*)—

Though with the weight of her heavy hips moving slowly in another direction,

She is, treading on my heart and making it heavy.

Vidushaka

We have seen what was here, worth-seeing. Now the heat of the midday sun, so to say, causes the fire of my hunger to blaze with redoubled fury. Let us therefore quit, so that I at least may be able to sustain myself by becoming a guest of the hermits and getting from them a humble food of roots and fruits.

Jimutavahana (*Looking at the sky*)

Oh, the sun has reached the zenith. For,—

This grand elephant is wearing the semblance of the unbearable state of a lonesome lover,

As his cheeks are very pale with the fresh sap of sandal tree againts which he has been rubbing to allay his heat,
As he is fanning his face with the caressing wafts of air stirred by his fan-like ears,

And he is drenching his chest with the spray discharged from his trunk.

End of the first act. (*Exeunt both*)

Second Act

Cheti (*Enter Maidservant*)

I have been bidden by princess Malayavati saying, "Manoharika, my girl, my brother Mitravasu is late in coming. So, go and find out if he has returned or not."

(*Goes. Looking toward the retiring room*)

Who be this, the girl who is hurrying this way ?

(*Observng closely*)

Oh, Chaturika ?

(*Enter Chaturika*)

Manoharika (*Approaching*)

Chaturika, my dear, what makes you come in such a hurry ?

Chaturika

Princess Malayavati, has ordered me saying "Chaturika my girl, my body is awfully tired with the exertion of plucking flowers and the heat is tormenting me as severly as the autumn sun. So, go and get ready the Chandrakanta (moonstone) bed in the sandal-bower shaded with the young leaves of plantain trees." I have done as ordered. I shall now go and inform the Princess.

Manoharika

If so, then be quick and inform her, so that by going there the torment of her heat my be alleviated.

Chaturika (*laughing, aside*)

Hers is not the kind of torment that can be relieved in this way. On the contrary, I am afraid, it will aggravate when she looks at the lonely sandal-bower and its loveliness.

(*Aloud*)

Well, you go now. I, too, shall go and report to the Princess that the Chandrakanta bed is ready.

End of Interlude (*Exeunt both*)

(*Enter Malayavati in love-lorn state, and the Maid*)

Malayavati (*Sighing, to herself*)

Alas, my heart ! having made me avoid that man out of modesty that day, now you have yourself gone to him. Ah, the selfishness of it !

(*Aloud*)

Girl, show me the way to the temple of Goddess.

Cheti

But, Princess, you had set out for the sandal-bower, I suppose ?

Malayavati (*Feeling abashed*)

You have well reminded me. Come, then let us go there.

Cheti

Come, come, Princess.

(*Leads the way*) (*Malayavati goes the ohter way*)

Cheti (*looking backward, to herself, in distress*)

Pity, how distracted she is ! What ! she is again going to the temple ?

(*Aloud*)

But the sandal-bower is on this side Princess. Come this way, Please.

Cheti (*Malayavati follows her, embarrassed and blushing*)

Princess, we have eome to the sandal-bower. Pray, enter it and refresh yourself by sitting on the moon-stone bed.

(*Both sit down*)

Malayavati (*Sighing aside*)

O God of love, him, who has outshone thee in splendour of beauty, thou has not even touched, but, on the other hand, taking me to be vulnerable as being the weaker one does not thou feel ashamed of thyself in smiting me, an innocent one.

(*Surveying herself and acting as if love-sick, aloud*)

Girl, how is it that this sandal-bower although sheltered from the sun by thick foliage as usual, does not alleviate the torment of heat today ?

Cheti (*With a smile*)

I know the cause of it, but Princess would deny it saying it was impossible.

Malayavati (*To herself*)

The girl has got it. I may, as well, ask her.

(*Aloud*)

What deuce you have to do with it ? Tell me, what the reason is.

Cheti

This, your, Vara=boon, husband, lover, so sweet to your heart.

Malayavati

(*Feels jubilant and rising up in excitement takes two or thoee steps forward*)

Where, where is he ?

Cheti (*Rising, with a smile*)

Princess, who do you say ?

(*Malayavati bashfully sits nown and keeps her looks downcast*)

Princess, what I meant to say was that, "The vision of the god Kama himself, lacking so to say only in his bow and arrow-which you forthwith saw when you dreamt that the Goddess had granted you the vara, so sweet to your heart, is the cause of your present affliction. "Tnat is why this sandal-bower though naturally cool, is inffective in mitigaing the torment of your heat today.

Malayavati (*Trimming the tresses of Chaturika*)

You are Indeed a clever girl, my Chaturika. How can I conceal the rest from you now ? I shall tell you all.

Cheti

Princess, you have already disclosed everything by your agitation at the mere mention of the word 'vara'. So, don't you fret now. If I am indeed Chaturika then even this has not escaped my notice. He, too, not seeing any more of you since, would not be taking interest in anything else even for a moment.

Malayavati (*In tears*)

How could I be so fortunate, my girl ?

Cheti

Don't say so, Princess. Could one ever imagine Vishnu finding peace without pressing Lakshmi close to his bosom ?

Malayavati

What else could a friend utter but that pleases ?

Friend, my torment is all the more severe for another reason also, that the gentleman, because I did not greet him even with a word, might have considered me uncouth.

Cheti (*She weeps*)

Do not weep, Princess.

(*Rising up she plucks a sandal leaf and crushing it she applies the juice to her breasts*)

I say, do not weep. Other wise, I am afraid, even this sandal juice that I am applying to your breasts, growing hot with the constant stream of your tears, won't alleviate your heart's torment.

(*Taking a plantain leaf, she beigns to fan her*)

Malayavati (*Pushing her away with her hand*)

Don't fan me, friend. The air of this plantain-leaf feels hot.

Cheti

Princess, don't blame this.

> You make the breeze of the plantain leaf hot by your sighs, Though the breeze be cool by contact with tender foliage of sandal trees.

Malayavati

Friend, is there any remedy for mitigating the torment ?

Cheti

Princess, there is. Only he should come here.

Jimutavahana (*Enter Jimutavahana and Vidushaka*)

I have already been the victim of her glancess,

Which produced the light and shade effect on the trees of the hermitage,

As if glisterning sables were hanging from their branches, She cast glances at me in the very presence of that hermit just as she turned.

Why then, O Kama are you shootiug your arrows at me in vain ?

Vidushaka

Where has your self-control fled, my friend ?

Jimutauahana

Why friend, I am quite self-controlled ! For,—

Have I not passed the moonlit nights, Haven't I smelt the blue lotuses

Have I not suffered the evening breezes laden with the fragrance of blooming jasmine ?

And haven't I listened to the humming of the bees over the lotus-pond ?

Then how, indeed, do you call me, one of the forlorn lovers, though I am lacking in self-control ?

Or may be, I am wrong in my defence.

Friend Atreya, when I have succumbed even to the mild, charge of the flowery arrows of the unsubstantial Kama how can boast of being brave ?

Vidushaka (*Aside*)

By confessing his weakness in this manner, he has only given vent to his pent up emotion. So I shall divert his mind to something else.

(*Aloud*)

Friend, how is it that you have returned so quickly from the service of the your parents ?

Jimutavahana

An apt question indeed, my friend. Whom else could I take into confidence ? Last night I had a dream in which I saw that very love of mine seated on the moon-stone slab here in this

(*Pointing with the finger*)

Sandal-bower and weeping as if chiding me for something in lover's quarrel. So I wish to pass this day in this very place which has become so dear to me on account of its being the rendezvous of my sweet-heart in my dream. Then come along, let us go there.

(*They go*)

Cheti (*Listening, with excitement*)

Princess, I hear something like the sound of footsteps.

Malayavati (*Surveying herself, with agitation*)

Friend, least somebody should read my heart from my present looks, we had better get up and hide behind the cover of this red Asoka to see who is coming.

(*They do so*)

Vidushaka Here is that sandal-bower. my friend. Come let us go in.

(*They gesticulate entering*)

Jimutavahana (*Having entered)*

This sandal-bower in spite of its moon-stone bench has no appeal for me

Without the presence of my moon-faced love, even as the evening without the light of the moon.

Cheti (*Seeing Jimutavahana*)

Congratulations, Princess ! It is he, so sweet to your heart.

Malayavati *Looking, with mingled joy and nervousness*)

My dear, seeing him so close, I feel too nervous to remain here. Perchance he sees me ! Come, let us go to some other place.

Cheti (*With a suppressed laughter)*

You, timid girl ! Who can possibly see you while you are here ? You conveniently forget that there is this red Asoka tree in between. So, we shall keep staying here.

(*They do so*)

Vidushaka *(Observing*)

O friend, this is that very. . . . .

Cheti (*Jimutavahana sighs tearfully*)

Princess, I hear the words, "This is that very, (I suspect they are talking about some girl)

Let us listen.

(***Both listen***)

Vidushaka (*Shakes him with the hand*)

My friend, this is that same moonstone bench.

Jimutavahana

Yes, my friend, you have observed right.

(*Indicating with the hand*)—

Yes; this is the moonstone bench on which I saw my sweet heart weeping and sobbing profusely at my delay.
With her wan face placed on her delicate left hand,
The slight tremour of her eyebrows however,
Betraying the suppressed anger she was feeling within.

Come, let us sit down on this very moon-stone bench.

Malayavati (*Reflecting*)

Who could possibly she be ?

Cheti

Princess, just as we are looking at him from behind cover, he may also have noticed you.

Malayavati

Quite possible. But then why should he speak with reference to some beloved angered in love ?

Cheti

Don't entertain such suspicions. Let us listen further.

Vidushaka (*Aside*)

The story hold him. Well, I shall egg him on. (Aloud) But, my friend, what did you say to her when you saw her weeping thus ?

Jimutavahana

Fiend, I said to her—

This moonstone slab at the rise of your moonface,
Seems to melt as it is bathing in your tears.

Malayati (*Angrily*)

Do you hear, Chaturika ? Is there anything more to be heard ?

(*In tears*)

Come, let us go.

Cheti (*Holding her by the hand*)

Not so, Princess. I, for one, can't believe that one who has seen you once can ever speak like this with reference to another girl. Let us therefore wait till the end of the story.

Jimutavahana

Friend, I feel like diverting myself by drawing a picture of her on this very slab. So fetch for me some pieces of red arsenic from the mountain-side here.

Vidushaka

By all means, as you command.

(*Exit*) (*Re-enter*)

Friend, you had asked only for one kind of pastels, but look, here I have brought five colours. Now you may draw.

Jimutavahana

Well, done my friend.

(*Taking the pieces and making the drawing on the beautiful slab, with a thrill of excitement*)

Friend, see :—

> Even the first glimpse of the outline of the beautiful face of my beloved with lips luscious like the bimba fruit, gives me solace,
>
> Like the crescent moon which shines gloriously on a cloudless sky (or is as bright as the full moon) and is delightful to the eyes.

(*Resumes drawing*)

Vidushaka (*Looking at it with curiosity*)

Friend, it is really wonderful that you could draw it so well even the model is not present !

Jimutavahana

Friend,—

> My imagination has already placed my beloved before me here.
>
> If I look at her and draw, what is there to wonder at ?

Malayavati (*Sighing in tears*)

Chaturika, the story has surely come to an end. Come, let us go and look for Mitravasu.

Cheti (*With dismay, aside*)

Alas, her tone tells, she has grown sick of life.

(*Aloud*)

Princess, Monoharika has already left for him. It is possible the Prince, Mitravasu himself may be coming here.

Mitravasu (*Enter Mitravasu*)

I have been bid by my father saying, Mitravasu, my son, we have observed Jimutavahana here at close quarters. He is a suitable match. You please go and propose the hand of Malayavati to him." I, on the other hand, out of great affection for my sister, am tornby conflicting feelings. For,—

> Jimutavahana is the crowning glory of the Vidyadhara family, He is young, wise and favourite of the good,
>
> He isnunsuprassed in beauty and is a man of valour, and he is possessed of learning and culture,
>
> But moved by compassion, he may at any moment sacrifice even his life for the sake of another being,
>
> I am awfully torn between the feelings of joy and sorrow while offering the hand of my sister to him.

And I hear that Jimutavahana is somewhere here in the sandal-grove near the temple of Gauri. Here is the sandal-grove. I shall just enter it.

(*Enters*)

Vidushaka (*Looking with a start*)

Friend, hurry to cover the picture with this plantain leaf. Here comes Mitravasu, the Siddha Prince. He may see this.

Mitravasu (*Approaching*)

Prince, Mitravasu greets you.

Jimutavahana (*Seeing*)

Welcome Mitravasu. Come, and take your seat here.

Cheti

Prince, Mitravasu has actually arrived here.

Malayavati

Good, I am glad.

Jimutavahana

Mitravasu, how fares his Majesty, the Siddha King, Visvavasu ?

Mitravasu

Father is in good health. And I have come to you with his message.

Jimutavahana

What are the orders of His Majesty ?

Malayavati

I would like to hear father's message.

Mitravasu

This is father's message. "I have a daughter, called Malayavati who is the life-spring as it were of the whole Siddha community, I beg to offer her hand to you. May you oblige me by accepting her."

Cheti (*With a mild laugh*)

Princess, why don't you get angry ?

Malayavati (*Stands looking to the ground with eager expectations and bashfulness*)

Don't be over jubilant, my girl ! You forget that his heart is set on some one else ?

Jimutavahana (*Aside*)

I am in a dilemma, my friend.

Vidushaka (*Aside*)

I know you are interested in none else save her. But dismiss him with some evasive answer.

Malayavati (*Angrly, aside to herself*)

Confound you, wretch, who doesn't know this ?

Jimutavahana

Mitravasu, who would not welcome such a worthy relationship with you ? But I am sorry to say a heart set on one cannot be diverted to another. You will excuse me therefore, if I do not venture to accept her hand.

Cheti (*Malayavati acts as if swooning*)

Compose yourself, Princess, just compose yourself.

Vidushaka

My dear sir, he has no free will in this matter. So, what is the good of requesting him ? You had better go to his elders and request them.

Mitravasu (*Aside*)

He is right in saying this. He will not dare go counter to the commitments of his parents. Luckily, his parents too are residing hear near this Gauri temple. So I shall go and get the proposal about Malayavati accepted through his parents.

(*Aloud*)

The prince alone knows best why he has declined to accept our offer.

Malayavati (*Indignantly*)

Why, I wonder, should Mitravasu go on pressing his suit when he has been slighted by a refusal ?

(*Surveying herself, in tears*)

What shall I do now with this wretched body of mine except to suffer it with the disgrace and torment of frustration ? I shall, therefore, kill myself on the spot by hanging from this red Asoka with the noose of the Atimukta creeper. So this is settled.

(*Aloud, with an uncanny smile*)

Girl, just see if Mitravasu has gone out of sight or not, so that I may also leave this place.

Cheti

As the Princess wishes.

(*Advancing a few steps*)

I suspect that her mind is a little unhinged. So, I shall not go Hidden from view, I shall watch from here what she intends to do.

Malayavati (*Rising up, looking in all directions, and taking the noose, in tears*)

Gauri, my Goddees, you have not shown me any favour in this life. Pray, order that in my next life I have not to suffer similar anguish again.

(*Puts the noose round her neck*)

Cheti (*Seeing, in alaram*)

Help ! help ! Princess is committing suicide by hanging.

Jimutavahana (*Approaching hastily*)

Where is she, where is she ?

Cheti

There, beneath the Asoka tree.

Jimutavahana (*Seeing with joy*)

Oh ! it is she, the girl of my dreams !

(*Seizing Malayavati by the hand and snatching away the noose*)

Don't, don't you do such a rash deed, my sweet girl !

Take away your delicate hand from the creeper, the hand,

Which I think could ill bear the strain of plucking even a flower,

How can it have the strength for fasterning a halter ?

Malayavati (*Timidly*)

Woe me, who could be this man ?

(*Seeing Jimutavahana, tries to release her hand in resentment*)

Let go my hand, man, let go. Who are you to prevent me ? Even for dying shall I have to get your permission first ?

Jimutavanana

No, I will not let go (For)—

How can I let go the guilty hand which has been caught
In the act of putting a noose round the neck worthy of wearing a pearl necklace ?

Vidushaka

Madam, what could be the cause of her attempt at suicide ?

Cheti (*Significantly*)

Why, who else but this, your friend here ?

Jimutavahana (*Regretfully*)

How have I been the cause of her attempt to kill herself ? I don't understand.

Vidushaka

Lady, tell me how is that ?

Cheti

It is like this. Hearing that she is not acceptable to your friend who rejected the propoeal of Mitravasu in favour of his sweet-heart, whose figure he has drawn here, she, consequently, losing all interest in life, did this.

Jimutavahana (*Joyfully, aside*)

What ! Is she then Malayavati, the daughter of Visvavasu ? Or, from where else could the crescent moon spring, if not from the ocean ? Ah me ! a slight misunderstanding on my part led to all this.

Vidushaka

Madam, if that be so, my friend stands exonerated. If you still entertain a doubt, you may go and see the slab for yourself.

Malayavati (*Looking at Jimutavahana with an expression of mingled joy and bashfulness, tries to wrest her hand from his grasp*)

Leave my hand, I say, leave my hand.

Jimutavahana (*Smiling*)

I shall not leave it until you have seen my sweet-heart sketched on the slab.

(*All go there*)

Vidushaka (*Removing the plantain leaf*)

This is his sweet-heart !

Malayavati (*Observing, aside, smiling*)

Chaturika, it looks as if I have been painted here !

Cheti (*Looking alternately at the picture and then at Malayavati*)

Madam, do you say "as if I have been painted ?" The likeness is so striking as one could hardly tell if it was Princess's is own reflection in the moon-stone or her picture !

Malayavati (*With a laugh*)

By showing the picture he has made me look guilty.

Vidushaka

Friend, the seal has now been put on your love marriage. Leave her hand, for some other girl is coming here in hot haste.

(*Jimutavahana lets it go*) (*Enter the other Cheti*)

Cheti (*Approaching hurriedly, in the excitement of joy*)

Princess, congratulations ! You have been accepted on behalf of Jimutavahana by his parents.

Vidushaka (*Dancing*)

So it is fulfilled—the wish of my dear friend. No, that of her ladyship. Or no, not either, but—

(*Acting as if eating*)

of me alone, Brahmana.

Cheti (*Addressing Malayati*)

Prince Mitravasu has ordered me saying, "As the marriage ceremony of Malayavati shall be performed to day, go and bring her here quickly." Come, let us go now.

Vidushaka

You are going away taking her along with you, And my friend shall have to remain here alone ?

Cheti

Don't be impatient, fellow. You will just have everything ready for your bath.

(*exit Malayavati with retinue, looking at Jimutavahana fondly and bashfully*)

(*Behind scenes a bard recites*)

Lending to Malaya hill the golden sheen of Meru with showers of yellow sandal powder,

Putting to shame the purple glow of the rising as well as the setting sun with the freshly strewn vermilion,

This world of Siddhas proclaim for your welfare the time of your nuptial ablutions,

By means of the songs of dancing women which are revishing on account of being mingled with the chime of their anklets.

Vidushaka (*Listening*)

Here come the bathing requisites, my friend.

Jimutavahana (*with joy*)

If so, my friend, why delay here ? Come, let us go. After making obeisance to father, we shall repair to the bath-room-,

> Among lovers, matching each other in beauty, mutual attachment, family status and age,
> Who fall in love at first sight, very few, I believe, are so lucky as to be united in wedlock.

End of The Second Act (*Exeunt both*)

Third Act

Vita (*Enter Vita, tipsy but neatly dressed, with wine cup in hand, and Cheta*)

One who drinks day and night and the other who unites people with their sweet-hearts—

Only these two, namely, Baldeva and Kamadeva respectively, are my gods.

What a happy life is mine, Sekharaka !—

Of whom the three are close associates ever, —on this bosom a mistrees, In his mouth, a pull of lotus-scented liquour; and on his head, a wreath of flowers !

(*Staggering*)
Who pushes me, he ? (With a guffaw)
I am sure, it is Navamalika who is pulling my leg.

Cheta

Master, Navamalika has not yet come.

Vita (*Angily*)

The marriage cermony of Malayavati was over early in the first watch of the night, Now that the day has dawned why has she not come ?

(*With a flash of joy*)

Oh! I see, the whole populace of Siddhas and Vidhyadharas are enjoying themselves carousing in the Kusumakara garden, each with his sweetheart, on this auspicious occasion of Malayavati's wedding. My Navamalika too, must be waiting there for me. So let me go there, for what is Sekharaka without a fresh wreath, a garland without jasmine, or a room without the bride ?

Cheta (*Walks with unsteady gait*)

Here is the garden. Let my master enter.

(*Both enter*)

Vidushaka (*Enter Vidushaka with a pair of shawls placed on his shoulders*)

I heard that my friend would be going to the Kusumakara garden. So let me also go there.

(*Walking about*)

Here is the garden. Let me go in.

(*Entering, acting as if attacked by bees*)

Why are these wicked bees rushing at me ?

(*Smelling his body*)

Oh, I see. As the dear friend of their son in-low, I have been anointed with great respect by Malayavati's relations with coloured and scented unguents, and a wreath of santana flowers has been placed on my head. Their excessive regard has turned into a curse for me at this moment. What shall I do now ? Or, let me wrap myself like a woman with this pair of shawls, which I have received as a gift from Malayavati, in such a manner so that it hangs lossely about me, and go with my face veiled wtih the upperpart of it. Then I shall see what harm these accursed bees, can do to me.

(*Goes*)

Vita (*Observing with delight*)

Look, boy, there goes Navamalika

(*Pointing with the finger, and laughing*)

just the other way, veiling her face in anger at my coming late. I shall, therefore, throw my arms around her neck and pacify her.

(*Suddenly approaching, throwing arms around the neck tries to offer a betel-leaf with lips*)

Vidushaka (*Indicating smell of liquor, stopping his nose and turning away his face*)

Having escaped with great difficulty from the clutches of one sort of stingers, I have fallen into the clutches of a yet worse stinker !

(*Supplicates by placing Vidushaka's feet on his head*)

Why, my love, why turn your face away in anger ?

Forgive me, Navamalika, forgive me.

Cheti (*Enter Cheti*)

I have been ordered by the mother of the princess, saying, "Maid Navamalika, go to the Kusumakara garden and tell the keeper Pallavika to decorate the Tamala avenue exquisitely well, to-day, for my son-in-law will go there with Malayavati." I have conveyed the orders to Pallavika. Now, I shall go and seek Sekharaka, my darling, who must be feeling disconsolate for having had to pass the night with out me.

(*Seeing*)

Here is Sekharaka.

(*Angrily*)

What ? he cajoles another lady-love !

Vita

> That same Sekharaka who, out of pride, knows not to humble himself before even Brahma,
>
> Vishnu and Mahesa, is now falling at thy feet, my dear Navamalika !

Vidushaka

You whoreson, you dog of a drunkard ! where is Navamalika here ?

Cheti (*Observing, with a smile*)

What a fun ! here is Sekharaka, fuddled with drink propitiat ing brother Atreya mistaking him for me. Now, I shall feign anger and make a fool of them both.

Cheta (*Shaking Sekharaka with his hand*)

Master, leave him, leave him. This is not Navamalika. There comes she, looking at you with eyes red with anger.

Cheti (*Approaching*)

Sekharaka, who is this girl with whom you are flirting ?

Vidushaka (*Putting off the veil*)

It's me the son of an unfortunate mother !

Vita (*Seeing Vidushaka*)

O, you red monkey, you dare to jest with me, Sekharaka ! Boy, hold him fast till I have appeased Navamalik.

Cheta

As my master commandi.

Vita (*Leaving off Vidushaka, falls on Cheti's feet*)

Forgive me, Navamalika, forgive me.

Vidushaka

It's time I should slip away.

(*Tries to run away*)

Cheta (*Seizes Vidushaka by his sacred thread, the thread sanps*)

Where to my red monkey, where to are you fleeing ?

(*Tightening his scarf round his neck, drags him*)

Sister Navamalika, have mercy on me and get me released,

Cheti (*Laughing*)

Yes, I will, Only if you place your head on the ground and fall at my feet !

Vidushaka (*Angrily*)

I, a friend of the Prince, and should fall at the feet of a girl like you ?

Cheti (*Threatening with her finger and smiling*)

Presently I shall make you fall. Sekharaka, come, get up. I am reconciled with you.

(*Throws arms round his neck*)

It is dear friend of the prince, our son-in-law's, that you have ill-treated. Mitravasu, our master may hear of it, and get angry, You should therefore make up with him by paying proper respects to him.

Vita

As my Navamalika commands.

(*Throwing arms round the neck of Vidushaka*)

Sir, I made fun of you because I knew that you belonged to our dear in laws.

(*Reeling*)

Do you think that Sekharaka is really drunk ? No more jesting now.

(*Makes a coil of his scarf and offers it as a seat*)

Let our dear relative take uis seat here.

Vidushaka

Luckily, the effect of liquor on him is somewhat subsided.

Vita (*Takes his seat*)

Navamalika, you come and sit down beside him, so that I may propitate you both together.

(*Cheti sits down with a laugh*)

Boy, fill this cup to the brim with fine wine.

(*Servant raises the cup and acts as if filling it*)

Vita (*Taking flowers from the wreath on his head, dropping them into the cup and kneeling down, offerr it to Navamalika*)

Navamalika, make it purer by sipping it, and affer it to him.

Cheti (*Smiling*)

Just as Sekharaka commands.

(*Does so*)

Vita (*Offering the cup to Vidushaka*)

Here is a drink, all the sweeter by virtue of its touch with Navamalika's lips, and which none else but Sekharaka has ever tasted before. Just have a sip of it. What greater honour than this could I do to you ?

Vidushaka (*With an embarrased smile*)

Remember, Sekharaka, I am a Brahmin.

Vita

If you are a Brahmin, where is then your holy thread ?

Vidushaka

But that snapped when the servant pulled it.

Cheti (*Laughng*)

If so, then please repeat at least some Vedic words.

Vidushaka

Madam, even my Vedic words have been spirited away by the smell of the spirit. Or, what is the good of arguing with you ?

Here, this Brahmin falls at your feet.

(Pretends to fall at her feet)

Cheti *(Laughing and preventing with both hands)*

No sir, don't don't do this. Sekharak, in sooth he is a Brahmin.

(Falls at Vidushaka' feet)

You won't be cross, sir, I hope. For, the joke was quite natural as should have suited the relations-in-law. Sekharaka, you should also propitiate him.

Vita

Yes, I will.

(Falling at Vidushaka's feet)

Pray, sir, excuse me for my misbehavior under the influence of liquor, so that I may be able to accompany Navamalika to the drinking party with an easy conscience.

Vidushaka

You are forgiven. Now you can go, and I too shall look for my friend.

Vita

Thank you sir.

Vidushaka *(Exeunt Vita with Navamalika, and the Servant)*

Thank God, the Brahmin has been spared an untimely death. Now, I shall take a bath in this lake and wash the taint of my contact with drunkards.

(Does so. Looking in front)

Here comes my friend in this very direction, holding the hand of Malayavati as if she were Goddes. Lakshmi incarnate. So, I had rather stay here.

(Remains where he is)

Jimutavahna *(Enter Jimutavahana with Malayavati and, cortege in order of rark)*

When looked at, she bends her gaze down. When I address her, she keeps silent.
On the bed she keeps aside, when forcibly embraced she trembles,

And when her friends leave our bed-room, she wants to go with them.

This new bride of mine has grown all the dearer to me these days, by her very perversity.

(*Looking at Malayavati*)

Malayavati, darling !—

That I have been observing silence by replying to all questions with a mere 'hum',

That I have been exposing my body to the torment of the moonlight blazing like forest-fire,

And that many a day and night I have been passing in contemplation of none else but thee—

It is the fruit of all this hard penance, my love, that I have been able to see this, your face at last !

Malayavati (*Aside*)

My girl, not only is he handsome, but knows to speak beautifully also.

Cheti (*Laughing*)

O, my captious lady, it is the simple truth. What flattery is there in it ?

Jimutavahana

Chaturika, show us the way to Kusumakara garden.

Cheti

Come, come, my lord.

Jimutavahana (*Going, addressing Malayavati*)

Take care, my dear, come steadily, For,—

The weight of thy swelling breasts is enough for your slender waist to bear, Then why this superfluous neklace ? Your thighs are already sagging under your massive hips, why need you this girdle ?

Your feet can hardly carry your plump thighs, how could they, these additional anklets ?

Your limbs are themselves more than ornaments for you, then why bear an extra burden of trinkets to irk yourself ?

Cheti

We have arrived at the Kusumakara garden. Let my lord enter it.

Jimutavahana (*All enter*) (*Entering*)

Oh, the loveliness of the Kusumakara garden ! For here,—

The dripping sap of the sandal wood trees cools the floor of the bower.

Yonder. the peacock (Blue-necked) is seen dancing to the tune of the murmuring fountains.

The water, released by the wheel and made yellow by the pollen of flowers swept by the rush of its current.
Flows rapidly, filling on its way, the basins of the trees.

And here—

The bees, making the bowers resonant with their humming songs,

Wafting a blend of perfumes from the polien of flowers,
Drinking to their fill the sweet honey in company of their mates,

Seem to be enjoying a regular drinking bout all round !

Vidushaka (*Approaching*)

Hail ! Victory to the Prince ! And prosperity to the Princess !

Jimutavahana

You are late my friend.

Vidushaka

No, my friend, I came quite early. But you could not find me here because I was busy strolling round, out of curiosity, to see the drinking bouts of Siddhas and Vidyadharas assembled on the auspicious occasion of your wedding. My friend may also come and have a look at them.

Jimutavahana

As you like it.

(*Looking all around, joyfully*)

Look, look !—

The Vidydharas, with their body anointed with sandal-paste, are wearing wreaths of Santanaka flowers

Their spotless dresses are irridescent with the flashes of of their jewelry.

Mixing freely with the Siddhas they are drinking

Under the shade of sandal trees the wines first tasted by their sweet hearts.

Come, let us also go to the Tamala avenue.

Vidushaka (*All walk around*)

Here is the Tamala avenue. There is the sandal bower. But I see that the face of her lady ship is a little faded with the heat of the autumn sun. She may sit down on this crystal bench.

Jimutavahana

Friend, You have observed rightly. For,—

The face of my darling, outshining the moon by the fairness of its cheeks,

Now glowing red with oppressiue heat, I am sure, is out to put the red lotus to shame.

(*Holding Malayavati by the hand*)

Let us sit here, darling.

(*All sit down*)

Jimutavahana (*Raising Malayavati's face and looking at it*)

Darling, in vain we have troubled you without curiosity to see the Kusumakara garden. For, I think—

The face, with eye-brows tremulous like the creepers and petal-red lips vying with the Patala flower

Is a real garden, the very Nandana (Indra's garden) on earth, while every garden other than this is a mere forest.

Cheti (*Smiling, addressing the Vidurhaka*)

Do you hear how she has been described ?

Vidushaka (*Smiling*)

Don't feel elated on that account, Chaturika. Handsome persons are not wating among us, too. But it is through envy that no body comes forward to depict us so well.

Cheti (*Smiling*)

Why, I shall put you in true colours, sir.

Vidushaka (*Joyfully*)

You make me alive ! Please, madam, do this favour to me, so that this man may not say again, "You are like this you are like that, you have a monkey's face, and so on."

Cheti

Sir, I saw you this morning with your eyes closed, drowsing after keeping awake for the wedding. How beautiful you looked then ! May you again sit in that pose now.

Cheti (*Vidushaka does so*) (*Aside*)

Now I shall blacken his face with the juice of Tamala leaves which is like the blue indigo juice.

(*Rising up, plucking leaves, acts as if crushing them*)
Jimutavahana (*Jimutavahana and Malayavati meanwhile keep looking at Vidushaka's face*)

You are lucky, my friend because you are thus painted in true colours before our eyes.

(*Cheti acts as if blackening Vidushaka's face with Tamala juice*)
(*Malayavati smilingly look at him, and then at Jimutavahana*)

Jimuiavahana

The flower of a smile, Oh my fair-eyed darling, is bursting on your leaf-like lips there,
While its fruit, as I look at it, has appeared on my eyes here.

Vidushaka

Madam, what have you done ?

Cheti

Only painted you in bright colours, sir.

Vidushaka (*Wiping his face with hand, looking at the hand, angrily taking up a stick, in a rage*)

O girl, we are with the royal family here ! How shall I punish you ?

(*Turning to Jimutavahana*)

Look here, sir ! I have been made a fool of, in your very presence by this misbegotten maid. What is the good of my staying here ? I had better go somewhere else.

Cheti

Revered Atreya has indeed grown angry with me. So I shall go and pacify him.

Malayavati

Chaturika, my girl ! you go away leaving me alone ?

Cheti (*Pointing to Jimutavahana, smiling*)

I wish you were alone like this for ever.

Jimutavahana (*Exti*)

This face of thine, my darling, grown red with the rays of the sun,

And displaying filaments of light radiating from the teeth,
Is truly like a lotus.

But one misses the bee sucking the honey from it.

(*Malayavati laughs and raises up her face*)
(*Jimutavahana repeats the same stanza—"This face of thine, etc."*)
Cheti (*Enter*) (*Approaching suddenly*)

Here is Mitravasu, the Siddha Prince, come to see the Prince on some business.

Jimutavahana

Darling, you may go home. I shall be back soon, after seeing Mitravasu.

Mitravasu

How dare I convey brazen-facedly the news to Jimutavahana that his kingdom has been annexed by the foe

Without having first vanquished the latter with all the forces at my command.

Nevertheless, it is not proper to go on the expedition without informing him. So I shall first inform him and then go.

Jimutavahana

Come, Mitravasu, take your seat here.

(*Mitravasu sits down*)

You scem to be exited ?

Mitravasu

How can a wretch like Matanga be the cause of excitement ?

Jimutavahana

What has Matanga done ?

Mitravasu

He has invited his own ruin by invading your territory.

Jimutavahana (*Joyfully aside*)

How I wish it were true !

Mitravasu

I am only awaiting orders from the prince for putting him to rout. What more shall I say but that,—

Sooner then they have got orders from you, the Siddho armies, covering the whole field of the sky with their air fleet rushing from all sides,

Turning the daylight into a gloom as it were by screening the sun from view,

Shall set out for battle and clear your territory of the headstrong foe

Who has terrorized your vassal chiefs by his degradations.

Or, there is no need for the army units.

Yau may take the wretched Matanga as dead, for I myself will be the death of him,

When drawing my bright sword I shall make a dash and fall upon him

In the battle-field and engage with him in a close combat,
Like a lion, with his mane glistening like a flashing sword, springing upon a wild elephant.

Jimutavahana (*Stopping his ears, aside*)

What a cruel ieea ! Or, shall say this.

(*Aloud*)

Mitravasu, it is but a trifle for you.

Far bigger exploits could be expected of you who are so powerful. But,—

How can such a one as I, who am always ready to sacrifice my life.

Out of compassion for the sake of others,

Even without waiting for the asking, give my approval
To a cruel slaughter for the sake of a kingdom ?

Besides, I harbour no enemity against anyone but carnal passions. But if you are really anxious to do a good turn to me, then you should rather pity that poor fellow who is a slave to his passions.

Mitravasu (*With indignation and a sneer*)

Why not pity him ? He will be excused as if he has been our great benefactor and deserves our sympathy !

Jimutavahana (*Aside*)

It is difficult to check him at this moment when his mind is in a fresh transport of rage. Anyway, let me try like this.

(*Aloud*)

Get, up, Mitravasu, Let us go in. There I shall give you my advice, for the day has come to a close. See,—

Ever engaged in removing the closure of seals from the face of the lotus

Ever delighting the whole world by flooding the quarters with his rays

As if solely engaged in fulfilling men's desires, and ever looked at by the Siddhas with loud songs of praise

The sun, even while it is setting, is the one laudable exemplar of all whose efforts are directed towards the good of others.

End of the third act (*Exent both*)

Fourth Act

Chamberlain (*Enter Chamberlian carrying a pair of wedding-shawls, and Porter*)

Maintaining order in the harem,

Guarding against stumbling at every step

With the help of a staff, I enfeebled by age, imitate the whole conduct of a king,

Who maintains order and guards his country.

Porter

Where have you set out, sir ?

Chamberlian

I have been ordered by Queen, Mother of Mitravasu, thus :—

"Chamberlain, for ten days daily you should take red clothes to Malayavati and my son-in-law." Now, where should I go first ? The Princess is in her father-in-law's Jimutavahana, I hear, has today gone to see the tide on the sea-shore in company with Prince Mitravasu. So I am at a loss ta decide if I should go to Malyavati or to the son-in-law.

Porter

Sir, you had better go to the Princess. May be, by this time the son-in-law has returned there.

Chamberlian

Sunanda, a good suggestion. But where are you going ?

Porter

I too have been commended by His Majesty Visvavasu thus:—

"Sunanda, go and tell Mitravasu that he should come home and select something suitable to the occasion of the new-moon festival tonight for presenting to Malayavati and the son-in-law". Well then, you go to the Princess and I go to call Mitravasu home.

End of Interlude (*Exeunt both)*

Jimutavahana (*Enter Jimutavahana and Mitravasu*)

Turf for a bed, smooth slab for a bench, foot of the great tree for a house,

Cool spring-water for a drink, roots and tubers for food, deer for companions,

All these amenities of life we get in the forest quite unsought for, yet there is one drawback that

Here, the place being beyond the reach of the beggar folk one has to pass a useless life, devoid of all opportunity of being helpful to others.

Mitravasu (*Looking upwards*)

Prince, make haste, make haste. It is time for the tide to rush in.

Jimutavahana (*Listening)*

Yes, you have rightly observed the signs,—

Surely, the tide is coming tossing on its crost a shore countless shells and conches,

For we hear the rising noise that deafens the ears

Make the vaults of all mountain caves and hills around echo with its terrible din

Which is aggravated by the loud roar of the squealing hippos.

Mitravasu

Prince, it is already come up. For see,

This tide of the sea, with its water rendered fragrant by the cud of sharks and hippos

Chewing the cloves, looks as if sparkling with the lustre of gems.

Therefore, let us get out of the range of the tide and walk on the path which runs along the hill-top.

Jimutavahana

Mitravasu, look, the summits of this mountain, heaped as they are with white masses of autumnal clouds are wearing the splendour of the snow-clad peaks of the Himalaya.

Mitravasu

They are not the summits of Malaya, Prince. They are the dumps of Naga skeletons.

Jimutavahana (*in distress*)

Woe me ! But what was the cause that led to this mass destruction ?

Mitrava su

Prince, they were not wholesale massacres.

Jimutavahana

Then whot else were they, Mitravasu ?

Mitravasu

Listen. Formerly Garuda used to eat Nagas everyday as his food, by splashing off the water of the ocean with the storm raised by the flapping of his wings and forcibly dragging them out from their home below the earth.

Jimutavahana (*In distress*)

Oh, how cruel ! What then ?

Mitarvasu

Then the Naga king fearing the total extinction of the Naga race approached Garuda with the request

Jimutavahana (*With a look of appreciation*)

"Pray, eat me ?", did he say ?

Mitravasu

No, Not that.

Jimutavahana

Then what else ?

Mitravasu

He said, "In dread of thy swoop thousands of Naga woman miscarry and the new-borns also die. If it goes on like this, the total extinction of our race will only harm your own interest for which you come down upon the Nether world. Accordingly, I propose to send one Naga everyday to you for food, if you sit on the beach." And Garuda, the king of birds, agreed to the proposal.

> They are the heaps of skeletons of those Nagas whom according to this agreement,
>
> The king of birds eats for his food everyday, one by one. They have been and will be accumulating all the time--past, present; and future,
>
> They appear like the snowy peaks of Himalaya.

Jimutavahana

Alas ! was this the way how the Naga king saved the lives of the Nagas ?—

> Among the two thousand of tongues of Sesha-naga was there not one
>
> With which he could say "for the sake of saving this one Naga today I offer myself to the foe of Nagas ?"

What a pity !—

> The fools, we, commit sins for the sake of this accursed body
>
> Which is a repository of all that is filthy, and which is thankless and mortal !

Alas, what unending calamity has befallen the Nagas !

(*To himself*)

Shall I be able to save the life of even one single Naga by offering my own body in lien of his ?

Porter (*Enter Porter*)

I have ascended the top of the hill.

(*Looking around*)

Ah, there stands Mitravasu, there, beside the son-in-law. I shall go there.

(*Approaching, bowing respectfully*)

Hail to the Princes !

Mitravasu

Sunanda. what brings you here ?

Porter (*Whispering in the ear*)

This is it

Mitravasu

Prince, father calls me.

Jimutavahana

Yes, Please, go.

Mitravasu

But I must warn the prince not to stay here long, through curiosity, for the place is full of dangers.

Jimutavahana (*Exeunt Mitravasu and Porter*)

Meanwhile, I should also go down-hill and have a look at the beach.

(*Walks about*) (*Behind the scences*)

Ha, Sankhachuda, my son! what! shall I have to see three being killed today before my very eyes?

Jimutavahana (*Listening*)

Ah, it appears to be the wail of a women in distress. So, I shall approach her and find out who she is and what is the cause of her fear.

(*Goes*)

(*Enter Sankachuda followed by an Old Woman crying, and a State Peon tucking under his arm a pair of red shawls*)

Old Woman (*In tears*)

Ha! Sankachuda, my son, what a fate; I have to see three being killed today before my very eyes!

(*Holding his chin*)

Robbed of this moon-like face, the Nether world shall become dark.

Sankhachuda

Mother, why do you afflict yourself so much with excessive grief ?

Old Woman (*Gazing, touching the limbs of her son*)

Ah! my son! how cruel of heartless Garuda to make a meal of your tender body which has never before seen the light of the sun.

Sankhachuda (*Throwing arms round his neck*)

Mother, control yourself and stop your lament. For, you must know that—

Everybeing that is born is always first taken hold by Mortality.

It is only afterwards that the Mother takes up the child even like a nurse. Where then, is the occassion for sorrow?

Old Woman

Ah son! wait, let me have a look at the face just for a moment.

Peon

Come along boy. What concern do you have with her babbling now? Overwhelmed by her affection, she little knows the sternness of our official duty.

Sankhachuda

My good man, I am just coming.

Peon (*Aside*)

I have brought Sankhachuda almost near the death-slab. Now handing over to him this pair of red shawls as the victim's token, I shall show him the slab.

Jimutavahana

Oh! here is that woman.

(*Seeing Sankchuda*)

and surely he, must be her son for whose sake she is bewailing.

(*Looking around*)

But I don't see any cause of fear anywhere about! Should I then go and ask her the cause of her fear ? Or no, their talk is still going on. Perhaps it may reveal something. Let me therefore listen from behind the tree.

Peon (*In tears, folding his hands*)

Sankhachuda, my boy, this is the command of His Majestry, So, I have to convey to you something which is so inhuman.

Sankhachuda

Tell me, sir.

Peon

His Majesty the king of Nagas orders you.

Sankhachuda (*Touching his head with folded hands, respectfully*)

What is the orders of His Majesty for me ?

Peon

"Wearing this pair of red shawls mount the death slab so that Garuda may, recognizing you by thy token of the victim's red cloth, seize and carry you away for his food."

Jimutavahana (*In tears*)

Alas, that Vasuki should desert this poor fellow like that !

Peon

Sankhachuda, now take this please.

(*Hands over the red cloth*)

Sankhachuda (*Respectfully*)

Give me

(*Takes and lifting it to his head honours it as a command of his master*)

Old Woman (*Seeing the red cloth in her son's hand, beating her breasts*)

Ah son ! this is that wrapper, the victim's token, at the sight of which my heart sinks. (Faints)

Peon

This is about the time Garuda arrives. I should, therefore, make haste to leave this place.

Sankhachuda (*exit*)

Take heart, mother, take heart.

Old Woman (*Recovering, tearfully*)

Ah, son! Ah my child! Oh, whom I obtained as a reward of a thousand prayers! Where shall I see you again ?

(*Throwing her arms round his neck, weeps*)

Jimutavahana (*In tears*)

Oh, how cruel of Garuda !

> Mercilessly eating this child who is clinging to his mother's lap
>
> While the bewildered old women is fainting again and again, shedding a constant stream of tears

And is wailing aloud crying, "who will save thee, my child ?" and casting helpless looks all around,

I believe that not only Garuda's beak but even his heart is made of stone.

Sankhachuda (*Wiping his mother's tears*)

Don't be overwhelmed, mother. Take heart, I say takes heart—

Old Woman (*In tears*)

How can I take heart, my son? Did our Naga King show any mercy on you and keep you back because you are the only son of a poor mother? Ovile Death! you too in this vast living world could think only of my son, so relentlessly ? Unfortunate that I am, I am wholly undone ! (Swoons)

Jimutavahana

If I cannot save the life of this poor lad who is in distress, who is standing on the verge of death,

And has been deserted by his kinsmen, of what use would be this life of mine ?

So let me approach them.

Sankhachuda

Mother, compose yourself.

Old Woman

Sankhachuda, my son, it is hard to have composure. When even the protector of the Naga-world, Lord Vasuki himself, has forsaken you, who else will save you?

Jimutavahana (*Approaching*)

Most surely, I will.

Old Woman (*Hurriedly covering her son with her own scarf, approaching Jimutavahana*)

O Garuda, son of Vinata! kill me. I have been assigned for thy food.

Jimutavahana (*In tears*)

O, the mother's affection :—

Seeing such anguish of this old woman on account of the affection for her son,

I feel that even the heartless Garuda, the natural foe of the Nagas, may show mercy.

Sankahchuda

Mother, don't be so frightened. He is not Garuda, the foe of Nagas. For, see,—

Where, is Garuda with his ferocious beak bespattered with blood gushing from the torn skull of a big Naga,

And where, this saintly person whose face indicates nature as cool as the moon!

Old Woman

Alas! my son, I am so much distracted by the thought of your impending death that I see everything as Garuda.

Jimutavahana

Don't be afraid, mother. I am a Vidhyadhara and have come here to save your son.

Old Woman (*Joyfully*)

Say this again and again, my son.

Jimutavahana

What use is my saying it over and over again? I will prove the veracity of it by my act itself.

Old Woman (*Placing folded hands on forehead*)

May you live long, my son!

Jimutavahana

Mother, then let me have this victim's token so that wrapping myself in it,

I may offer myself to the son of Vinata (Garuda) for food to save the life of your son.

Old Woman (*Stopping her ears*)

God fodbid! Why you are as good a son to me as Sankhachuda, No, even more than Sankhachuda, as you wish to save my son who is abandoned by his kinsmen, by offering your own body.

Sankhachuda (*Smiling*)

How different from the world are the ways of this great soul! For,—

For sustaining which Visvamitra in olden times ate a dog's flesh like a Chandala,

For the sake of which Gautama killed Nadijangha who had been his benefactor,

And for preserving which this Garuda, the son of Kasyaya, daily feasts upon Nagas,

That same life, he gives up like a straw, out of pity for another, how wonderfull.

(*Addressing Jimutavahana*)

Noble soul, by your readiness to sacrifice yourself, you have indeed shown what genuine sympathy you feel for me. Now, please do not be too insistent. For,—

Petty creatures like me are born and they die.

But how rarely, comes a soul like thee who is pledged to self sacrifice, so why should you press this ?

Jimutavahana (*Holding Sankhachuda by the hand*)

Sankhachuda, my boy, you should not put obstacles in the way of my anxiety to serve the interests of others for which this opportunity has come to me as godsend after a long time.

(*Falling at his feet*)

Don't you hesitate now, hand me over the victim's token.

Sankhachuda

Noble man, what is the good of this futile endeavour ? Sankhachuda is not going to sully his Sankhapala family which is as immaculate as a conch. If still you are dctermined to show compassion on us, then please think of some way by which my mother is saved from dying by the shock of this catastrophe.

Jimutavahana

What is there to think of ? I have already thought of the way. Its success lies in your hands.

Sankhachuda

What is that, if I may hear ?

Jimutavahana

She is sure to die if you die, but she can live if you continue to live.

If you are anxious to see her live, then save your own life with mine.

This is the way out. So be quick and hand over the victim's token to me so that I may wrap myself in it and mount the death slab. You, take your mother along with you and quit this place, lest by merely seeing the place of execution close at hand, she should with her faint heart give up the ghost. Don't you see these vast funeral grounds littered all over with the skulls and bones of the dead Nagas ? For see,—

Here on these grounds, which are overcast with a thick gloom coused by the flutter of the wings of vultures,

Hovering with increased avidity to eat the bits of flesh torn by and half falling from their nibbling beaks,

The flames of the fire-brands dropped from the mouths of jackals,

Are hissing themselves out in the pool of blood, reeking with the smell of fat which is flowing so copiously.

Sankhachuda

How could I fail to see it ?—

These funeral grounds with their heaps of bones and skulls bathed white in the moonlight affording pleasure to Garuda (Vinayaka) by serving him with a Naga for food everyday without fail look as hideous to me as the body of Rudra adorned with skulls and bones

Flashing in the light of his crescent, affords delight, skulls and bones flashing in the light of his crescent,

Afford delight to Ganesa with its serpent wreaths that never fail, to bedeck it.

You had better go away. Why frighten me like this ? The time of Garuda's approach is drawing near.

(*Kneeling before his mother, touching his head with folded hand*)

Mother, you should also now return,—

In whatever form of life I may be re-born,

O fond mother, may thou be my mother always.

(*Falls at her face*)

Old Woman (*In tears, aside*)

O, this was to be the last wish of his !

(*Aloud*)

Son, my steps fail me when I have to go away leaving you here. I will accompany you rather.

Sankhachuda (*Rising*)

Meanwhile, let me go and do homage to Lord Dakhina Gokarna, whose temple is not far away, before obeying the orders of my master.

Jimutvahana (*Exit with his mother*)

Alas ! my wish could not be fulfilled. What can I do now ?

Chamberlain (*Entering suddenly*)

This pair of shawls—........

Jimutavahana (*Joyfully, Seeing, to himself*)

Thank God, this pair of red shawls, arrived so unexpectedly, has, so to say, fulfilled my wish.

Chamberlain

This pair of shawls has been sent for the Prince by the Queen, Mitravasu's mother. The Prince may wear it.

Jimutavahana

Bring it to me.

(*Chamberlain hands it over, aside*)

My wedding, Malayavati, has borne its fruit.

(*Wearing, aloud*)

Chamberlain, you may go now. Pay my respects to the mother Queen.

Chamberlain As the Prince commands.

Jimutavahana (*Exit*)

> This pair of red shawls, having come at the opportune time fills me with ineffable joy
>
> As I am about to sacrifice my life for the sake of another.

(*Looking in all direction*)

From the impetuous gale that has broken out, shaking the rocks on the top of Malaya hills, I conclude that Garuda has come very near. For,—

> His spreading wings are filling the firmament as if it were over cast with the clouds of doomsday.
>
> The water of the sea, tossed by his swoop is breaking on shore as if to deluge the earth.

Dazzling like the twelve suns risen simultaneously, he is blazing all the ten quarters with the luster af his body

And is being gazed at with fear by the guardian elephants of quarters, apprehensive of the day of Destruction.

But I should be quicker to ascent this death-slab before Sankhachuda arrives.

(*Doing so, sitting, and indicating the feel of it*)

O, how pleasant it feels :—

Not even the touch of Malayavati's body anointed with fresh sandal paste is so soothing

As that of this death slab leading to the fulfilment of my wish,

Or, why speak of Malayavati ?—

Even while lying snug in the lap of my mother I had'nt enjoyed that pleasure in my childhood

Which I am now getting from the contact of this death-slab.

Lo, there is Garuda—arrived ! So, let me wrap myself and wait. (*Does so*)

Garuda (*Enter Garuda*)

Look ! here,—

In an instant I have come to the sea-side hills of Malaya, avid for my meal of a Naga,

With the span of my wings extended by the clouds clinging to their ends.

Being watched with interest by my elder brother as the steeds of sun's chariot shied

And he strayed from his course causing Seshanaga to coil up in fear, and brushing the puny moon aside.

Jimutavahana

In every existence in which I be re-born again and again, may my body, by virtue of the merit I am going to acquire by saving the life of a Naga

At the cost of my own today, be dedicated everytime in a like manner to the good of others.

Garuda (*Seeing Jimutavahana*)

Lo ! with a sudden swoop, now I am going to rip open with my beak, which is harder than thunder bolt,

The chest of this Naga who is lying in this death-slab to save the lives of his fellow Nagas,

And carry him away for my meal, wrapped as he is in red clothes.

And is looking as if he were bathed in the stream of blood flowing from his heart rent by dread of me,

(*Swoops and lift up Jimutavahana. Shower of flowevs, and drum sounds behind the curtain. Looking up and listening*)

Oh, a shower of flowers and the music of drums !

What ! Is this really a shower of flowers that is falling from the sky and attracting the bees with its sweet smell ? And is this, music of drums in Heaven filling the quarters with its peal ?

(*Laughing*)

I see ! It must be the Parijatha tree of Heaven, which has been shaken by the storm raised by my impetuous flight.

This noise must have been caused by the Clouds of Destruction in anticipation of Dissolution.

Jimutavahana (*Aside*)

Luckily, my object has been fulfilled.

Garuda (*feeling the weight*)

As this saviour of the Nagas feels Guru (Substantial),

I am sure he shall cancel my craving for the Naga-meal today. Now, I shall ascend the Malaya summit and make a hearty meal of him.

End of the Fourth Act (*Exit carrying Jtmutavahana*)

Fifth Act

Porter (*Enter Porter*)

Even when a dear one is gone only to the garden of one's own house, affection fills the heart with misgivings,

How much more would it do so, when he is away somewhere in a dreadful forest infested with many dangers.

For, His Majesty Visvavasu is feeling ill at ease at the delay the Prince Jimutavahana is making in returning from the seaside where he had gone eager to see the tide. His Majesty has bid me thus. "Sunanda, the report that dear Jimutavahana, my son-in-law, is gone to that notorious place haunted by Garuda and is delaying to come back, has made me apprehensive. Therefore, hurry to that place and bring me the news whether he has returned home or not." Accordingly, I am going there.

(*Walking about, looking ahead*)

Oh, there is Jimutaketu, Prince Jimutavahanas father sitting in the courtyard of his cottage and being attended upon by his wife and his daughter-in-law Malayavati. There,—

Wearing a pair of white silken shawls, frilled at the border, falling in folds,

And accompanied by his highly virtuous wife, as old as himself,

Jimutaketu presents the grandeur of the ocean with its surface ruffled by the waves bearing foam on their erests, near the holy Ganges,

Near him shines Malayavati like the sea shore near Malaya mountain.

Let me approach him.

Jimutaketu (*Enter Jimutaketu seated, with wife and daughter-in-law*)

I have had my fill of youth's pleasures, and spread far and wide,

I have ruled firmly over a kidgdom, I have also performed penance,

I have a worthy son, and this daughter-in-law of mine also comes of an equally high family,

Having thus lived a full life, I have no other care than to think of death.

Porter (*Approaching suddenly*)

Of Jimutavahana.

Jimutaketu (*Stopping his ears*)

God forbid !

Old Queen

May the evil word be averted '

Malayavati

This bad omen makes my heart shudder.

Jimutaketu

Good man, what of Jimutavahana ?

Porter

Of Jimutavahana I have to hear the news from you. For which purpose, I have been sent here by His Majesty Visvavasu. Your Majesty may, therefore, please command me what I should convey to my master.

Jimutaketu

What ! is my son not there ?

Old Queen (*Shocked*)

My lord, if he is not there also, where could my child have gone, that he should be tarrying so long ?

Jimutaketu

He must have strayed far in search of provision for us.

Malayavati (*Dejectedly, Aside*)

I, for my part, not seeing my lord even for a moment begin to have serious misgivings.

Porter

Command me, sir, as to what I am to convey to my master.

Jimutaketu (*Indicating throbbing of the left eye*)

While I am worried over why Jimutavahana is delaying,

Why dost thou, O left eye, throb again and again foreboding ill to me.

Devil take thy throbbing, wretched eye, may child be safe !

(*Looking upwards*)

That venerable god, Sun, who is the eye of the world, Shall see to the welfare of Jimutavahana with the fiash of his light.

(*With a start*)

What is it that is falling so rapidly from the sky,
Dripping blood and blinding the sight like a molten meteor
At the time of Destruction, dazzling the eyes of the spectator

And leaving behind a red trail of light.
Oh, it has fallen at my feet !

Jimutaketu (*All stare at it*)

Look ! it is a crown to which fresh bits of flesh and hair are sticking. Whose possibly could it be ?

Old Queen (*Sadly*)

This jewelled crown looks like that of my child !

Malayavati

Don't say so, mother.

Porter

Your Majesty, don't be despondent without knowing it for certain. For,—

Such crowns belonging to the Nagas assigned for Garuda's food,
Falling down like meteors, are a matter of daily phenomenon here.

Jimutaketu

Queen, what he says, is sensible. It is quite possible.

Old Queen

Sunanda, I presume that by this late hour my child may have arrived at the house of his in-laws. There fore, go and without wasting a moment bring us the happy news.

Porter

As Her Majesty commands.

Jimutaketu (*Exit*)

Queen, supposing it is the crown of a Naga ?

Enter Sankhachuda wrapped in red clothe)

Sankhachuda (*In tears*)

Alas, alas !

As soon as I returned to the execution-ground of the Nagas after hurriedly making obeisance to Lord Gokarna on the beach,

Lo! Garuda flew away carrying that bleeding Vidyadhara, whose chest he had ripped open with his beak and talons.

Oh, my only selfless friend ! Oh, thou, the most merciful of all ! Oh, thou who didst take others' sufferings to heart ! Where are you gone ? Vouchsafe me an answer. Ah, Sankhachuda, wretch ! What have you done ?

Neither did I earn a good name by saving the life of a Naga, nor to my credit carry out the orders of my master.

On the contrary, for having been saved by another at the cost of his own life, I have become the object of worst pity. Woe is me, I am undone, I am undone !

In these circumstances, I cannot stand this life of shame even for a moment. I shall therefore try to follow him.

(*Walking around, staring at the ground*)

Let me closely follow this trail of blood in search of Garuda

The trail which is thick at the start on account of profuse flow of blood,

Gradually reduced to thin drops on account of intermittent falling then shattered to atoms by splashing on the boulders,

Infested with ants on the earth and hardly visible on red mineral rocks and top of thick trees, and appearing clotted in pits.

(*Walks about*)

Old Queen (*With fear*)

My lord, my heart sinks at the sight of that stranger who is coming here with hurried steps and a glum look on his face. Let us enquire who he is.

Jimutaketu

As the Queen says.

Sankhachuda (*Crying bitterly*)

O, you, the one crown of the three worlds ! Where are you lost ? Where shall I find you ? I have been robbed, I have been robbed !

Jimutaketu (*hearing, joyfully*)

My queen, don't grieve any more. This crown belongs to him. It must have been plucked off by some greedy bird from his head mistaking it for a piece of flesh, and fallen here while being carried.

Old Queen (*Embracing Malayavati in a fit of joy*)

Take heart, my girl, you are lucky. Your husband is safe ! Yours is not the age which should know the sorrows of widowhood.

Malayavati (*Joyfully*)

Mother I take it as your blessings.

(*Falls at her feet*)

Jimutaketu (*Approaching Sankhachuda*)

Child, has your crown been lost ?

Sankhachuda

Father, not mine alone but of all the three worlds.

Jimutaketu

How ?

Sankhashuda

At the moment I am so much chocked with grief that I cannot speak.

Jimutaketu (*Aside*)

Oh, I am ruined !

(*Aloud*)

Tell me, my son, of thy overwhelming grief

So that by being shared with me it may become a little bearable to you.

Sankhachuda

Then listen. I am a Naga. named Sankhachuda, who was, in turn, sent by Vasuki to Garuda for his food. But how can I go on with my story at length when I am afraid that this trail of blood may disappear from view under dust. To cut short—

> One of the Vidhyadharas, whose heart was moved with compassion for me,
> Offered himself to Garuda and saved my life.

Jimutaketu (*Dejectedly*)

Who else could be so anxious for doing good to others ? Why not say plainly it was my son Jimutavahana who did it ? O, I'm undone !

Old Queen

O, my son ! What have you done ?

Malayavati

O, that my misgivings should have thus come true !

(*All swoon*)

Sankhachuda (*In tears*)

Surely, they are the parents of that noble man, who have been reduced to this plight by my breaking the ill news to them. Or why, what else but venom can fall from the myuth of an adder ? What a befitting return has been made by Sankhachuda to Jimutavahana, the saviour of his life ! Then, should I kill myself on the spot ? No, Let me first revive them. Take heart, father ! Take heart mother !

(*Both recover consciousness*)

Jimutavahana ? Then, why are you wailing so plaintively ?

Malayavati (*Falling at his feet, with folded hands*)

Father, hand over the crown of my lord to me so that clasping it to my heart I may enter into the funeral pyre and end my pain for ever.

Jimutaketu (*In taers*)

My virtuous daughter, why do you over whelm me so much, with grief, when all of us have made the same resolve ?

Old Queen

Then why wait, my lord ?

Jimutaketu

Not at all, Queen. But house-holders are not enjoined to be cremated with any other than the sacrificial fire. So let us fetch fires from the sacrificial grounds and burn ourselves.

Sankhachuda (*Aside*)

Alas, for the sake of a single wretch like me, this whole Vidhyadhara family would perish ! let me say this.

(*Aloud*)

Old father, it is not advisable to take such a rash step without ascertaining the facts. The ways of Fate are strange. It is quite possible that the sworn enemy of Nagas, Garuda, discovering that is not a Naga, may let Jimutavahana go alive. So come, let us follow the track of Garuda along this very trail of blood.

Old Queen

Wholly by the grace of gods may I see my son alive !

Malayavati (*Aside*)

Little hope of luck for a wretched creature like me.

Jimutaketu

Son, would these words of thine come true ! Still, it is only proper that we go carrying fire along with us. So, thou follow the trail and we will be just on your heels, bringing sacred fires from the sacrificial shed.

Sankhachuda (*Exit with wife and daughter-in-law*)

Well, let me now follow Garuda.

(*Walking about, observing in the distance*)

> There, from this distance, can be seen Garuda, the enemy of Nagas seated on the summit of Malaya,
>
> Making pits on the surface of the rock by rubbling on it frequently his blood-stained beak,
>
> Singeing the neighbouring woods with the flames shot from his flashing cyes,
>
> And gripping vice-like the earth by digging into it the ends of his formidable and adamant-hard talons.

(*Enter Garuda seated, with Jimutavahana laid in front*)

Garuda (*To himself*)

Ah ! ever since my birth, the time I began eating Nagas, I have never before come across such a wonder as this that this noble soul not only does not wince under pain but instead seems happy. For,—

> Although I am sucking more and more blood out of him, this noble soul seems a veritable ocean of fortitude,

He shows no sign of wincing. His face is beaming with delight even under the excruciating pain of picking flesh ! The part of his body, which has not yet been devoured, shows visible horripilation !

And the look he casts on me is full of gratitude as if I were his benefactor rather than a wrong-doer as I actually am !

By his equanimity, he has excited my curiosity. I shall stop eating him, and find out who he is.

(*Draws away*)

Jimutavahana (*Seeing him disinclined to pick fiesh*)

Blood still runs from the ends of my veins,

Garuda (*Aside*)

O, wonderfull, even in this plight he speaks such magnificent words !

(*Aloud*)

With my beak I have only succeeded in drawing blood out of your heart,

But by this fortitude of yours you have drawn the very heart out of me.

I am, therefore, anxious to know who you are.

Jimutavahana

You are hardly in a fit state to it because you are oppressed by hunger. So, you should first satiate yourself with my flesh and blood.

Sankhachuda (*Approaching suddenly*)

Don't do this rash act ! He is not a Naga. Leave him and eat me. It was sent by Vasuki, as thy meal.

(*Opens his chest and offers*)

Jimutavahana (*Seeing Sankhachuda, in dismay, aside*)

Alas ! the arrival of Sankhachuda has thwarted my wish.

Garuda (*Surveying both*)

Both of you wear the victim's token. I can't make out which of you is a Naga.

Sankhachuda

Your doubt is ill-founded. For,—

Let alone the Svastika mark on my chest, can't you see the slough on my body ?

Could you not even count my two tongues while I spoke ?

Don't you see these three hoods of mine which expand while I hiss with unbearable grief

Whose crest-jewels have been besmirched by the cloud of smoke arising from the blaze of my venom ?

Garuda (*Looking at the hoods of Sankhachuda and then at Jimutavahana*)

Oh, then who is it that I have killed ?

Sankhachuda

He is Jimutavahana, the glory of the Vidhyadhara race. How merciiess of you that you have perpetrated so cruel a thing !

Garuda

Oh, this is he, Jimutavahana, that well-known Prince of the Vidhyadharas ?—

Whose praise I have often heard sung by minstrels wandering on the Lokaloka mountain,

On Meru, in the caves of Mandara, on the peaks of Himalaya,

On the mountain Mahendra, on the cliffs of Kailasa,

And even on the table lands of Malaya.

I am cought in the mire of infamy.

Jimutavahana

O, my noble Naga ! why do you feel so depressed ?

Sankhachuda

Is it not the occasion for feeling depressed ? Tell me,

Does it become you to sink me even lower than the depths of the Netherworld

By thus saving my life from Garuda by offering your own instead ?

Garuda

O, this noble man, with his heart moved by campassion, in order to save the life of a Naga has almost fallen into my jaws, voluntarily offered himself for my meal ! Thus, I have committed a great sin. In short, I have killed the very Bodhisattva. So, of this heinous sin, I see no other expiation than plunging into the fire. But where to find fire ?

(*Looking in all directions*)

O, here are some people coming in this very direction carrying fire in their hand. Let me, in the meanwhile, wait for them.

Sankhachuda

Prince, your parents have come.

Jimutavahana (*ill a ease*)

Sankhachuda, come here, Sit by me and, covering my body with this scarf, hold me up with your support, lest my mother, seeing me in this condition, should instanly die.

(*Sankhchauda, taking up the scarf lying beside, does so*)
(*Enter Jimutaketu with wife and daughter-in-law*)

Jimutaketu (*in tears*)

O my son, Jimutavahana :—

True, that the ways of Mercy know no distinction between one's own and a stranger.

But, how is it that the question whether you should save many or only one never occured to you

For' by sacrificing your own life to save one Naga from the clutches of Garuda,

You have exterminated your own self, your parents and your wife-our whole family.

Old Queen (*Addressing Malayavati*)

My child, control your emotion just for a moment. See, these tears of yours are extinguishing the fire.

(*All Walk about*)

'Garuda' O, my son, Jimutavahana"—so he cries ! certainly he must be his father. Let alone his fire. I cannot even show him my face out of sheer shame of having killed his son. Or, why should I be worried for want of fire, when I am sitting on the sea-coasts ? Nowlo :—

I am going to plunge into this submarine Fire at hand which is as terrific as the fire of Destruction which,

When kindled with the blasts of air, more violent then the havoc-making gusts of the whirldwind, stirred by my wings,

Is capable of consuming the seven seas like a drop of ghee by means of its fast-spreading flames

That are comparable to the tongues of death lolling with the gusto of devouring the three worlds.

Jimutavahana (*About to rise*)

O king of Birds, withhold thyself from this desperate step. This is no atonement of the sin thou hast committed.

Garuda (*Kneeling down, with folded hands*)

Then what else is, pray tell me, noble sir ?

Jimutavahana

Wait for a while. My parents have arrived. Let me first pay them my respects.

Garuda

By all means.

Jimutaketu (*Seeing joyfully*)

Congratulations, my Queen ! Here is our child Jimutavahana, who is not only alive but is being honoured by Garuda, sitting in front with hands folded like an obedient pupil.

Old Queen

My lord, I am really lucky to have been able to see the face of my child, who is hale and hearty.

Malayavati

True, though I see my lord before me, I cannot believe my eyes thinking it was impossible !

Jimutaketu (*Approaching*)

Come, my child, come and cling close to my heart.

(*Jimutavahana trying to rise, his scarf slips and he faints*)

Sankhachuda Prince, hold thyself up, hold thyself up !

Jimutaketu Ah, son ! even after seeing me thou hast gone away leaving me behind, thus ?

Old Queen

O, my child ! thou didst not accost me even with a word of greeting ?

Malayavati

Ha, my lord ! How is it even your parents are to be neglected by you ? (*All swoon*)

Sankhachuda

Oh, wretched Sankhachuda ! Why could not you die before you were born, that every moment you nave to bear this agony worse than death ?

Garuda

All this mess is the result of thoughtlessness on my part, who am so cruel. Let me do this much at least.

(*Fanning with wings*)

Recover thyself, my noble man, recover.

Jimutavahana (*Recovering*)

Sankhachuda, bring my parents back to consciousness.

Sankhachuda

Revive, old father ! revive. Revive, mother ! revive Jimutavahana has recovered himself. Don't you see that he has sat up only to bring you back to consciousness ?

Old Queen (*Both revive*)

O my son ! that you should be thus snatched away from us by the cursed Death before our very eyes !

Jimutaketu

Queen, don't utter such ominous words. He is alive, our dear son, May he live long ! You had rather look to the recovery of our daughter-in-law.

Old Queen (*Covering her face with scarf, siill weeping*)

May the evil be averted ! I will not weep. My Daughter ! Recover yourself. Better have a look at your husband while he is alive.

Malayavati (*Recovering herself*)

Ah, my lord ! What is an unluckly woman like me to do now ?

Old Queen (*Wiping Malayavati's face with her hand*)

My child, don't lose heart like this. It is inauspicious.

Jimutaketu (*In tears*)

Seeing the life of my son come to the last gasp in the
throat for lock of sustenance anywhere else,

the rest of the body having been consumed away-why the wretch that I am do not shatter into a thousand pieces ?

Malayavati

How hard-hearted indeed am I, that seeing my lord in such agony, I do not die at once.

Old Queen (*Feeling Jimutavahana's limbs, addressing Garuda*)

Ah, brute ! this is how you have mangled the body of my son which was full of splendour of fresh youth ?

Jimutavahana

Don't say so, mother. What has he done to it ? For, it was already in fact like this before—

What beauty is there in this so-called body which is merely a lumb of fat, bone, marrow, flesh

And blood covered over with skin, ever so loathsome to behold ?

Garnda

Noble sir, hard is my lot. I consider myself engulfed in the flames of Hell-fire. Advise me how I can absolve myself of this sin ?

Jimutavahana

Pray, father, allow me to tell him the atonement of his sin.

Jimutaketu

Do so, my child.

Jimutavahana

O Garuda, listen.

Garuda (*Kneeling before him, with folded hands*)

Bid me, master.

Jimntavahana

Withhold yourself from this regular killing of beings, Feel penitent for what you have already done.

Accumulate merit with assiduity granting security of life to all, so much so that sunk into it, the sin,

That clings to you on account of this small slaughter bears no bitter fruit,

Like unto a bit of salt thrown into a lake with fathomless and endless expanse of water.

Garuda

Roused by thee to wakefulness from the slumber of my ignorance,

Here I pledge myself to abstain from the killing of all life for good.

Now,—

Let the community of Nagas romp about at will in the ocean,
Here forming themselves into an island by spreading out their hoods like an expanse of sands,
Here creating the illusion of a whirlpool by coiling their bodies,
And there going from one coast to the other and making a causeway as it were.

And—

May the women-folk of Nagas in this grove of sandal-wood trees sing lustily the songs of your glory,
With their loosened locks of jet-black hair looking like heaped darkness and touching their heels,
With their cheeks aglow with the touch of the first rays of the sun as if with a dash of vermilion,
Heedless of the pain of their limbs languishing from exertion.

Jimutavahana

Bravo, my good man, bravo. I commend it. Now, be firm in your resolve, ever.

(*Addressing Sankhachuda*)

And you go to your house.

(*Heaving a sigh Sankhachuda stands with bowed head*)

Jimutavahana (*Singhing and looking at his mother*)

There, your mother must be in great anguish, every moment lamenting thy torment,
Thinking you torn by this time by the sharp beak of

Old Queen

Blessed is she who would see her son return whole from out of the jaws of Garuda.

Sankhachuda

This will be true only if and when the Prince revives.

Jimutavahana (*Indicating pain*)

Oh, the pain which I had not so long felt being lost in the enjoyment of the immortal joy that comes to one from the service of one's fellow beings—has now begun to afflict me.

(*Shows signs of sinking*)

Jimutaketu (*In alram*)

Oh, my child, why are you in such throes ?

Old Queen

Woe me, what is this ?

(*Beating her breasts*)

Help ! Help ! here my child is dying !

Malayavati

Oh, my lord, it looks, you are leaving me !

Jimutavahana (*Trying to fold hnds*)

Sankhachuda, pray bring my hands together.

Sankhachuda (*Doing so, in tears*)

Oh, the world becomes orphan !

Jimutavahana (*Looking at his parents with half-open eyes*)

This is my last obeisance,—

> My limbs are becoming numb and do not move, my ears fail to catch words though uttered clearly, alas !
>
> My eyes, too, are losing their sight all at once. Ah father! my life is departing in my utter helplessness.

Or why lament it ?

(*Falls down reciting a previous verse*)

By merit that today I earn—

by saving one Naga life spurning mine,
In every future life be't so to serve mine fellow beings,

Old Queen

Alas, my child ! Ah you, apple of the parents' eye Ah, Jimutavahana! Where shall I see you again ?

Jimutaketu (*In tears*)

Ah, my son, Jimutavahana ? Ah, darling of all dear ones ! Ah, you home of all virtues ? where are you ? Give me an answer !

(*Throwing up his arms in despair*)
Alas, O Alas !

Fortitude has lost its stay. Where shall Politeness find a refuge ?

Who is there to give prop to Forbearance ? Lost is Generosity !

Truthfulness is gone indeed ! Where shall poor compassion now go ?

The whole world has become void at thy departure, my son !

Malayavati (*In tears*)

Why, my lord, have you departed, leaving me behind ? Cruel Malayavati, was it to witness this, that you lived so long ?

Sankhachuda

Frince, where havc you gone leaving me, your slave, behind, whom you had treated dearer than life ? This Sankhachuda must follow you.

Garuda (*With emotion*)

Ha, the noble soul is no more ! What is it that I can do now ?

Old Queen (*In tears, looking upwards*)

O, Guardians of the worlds, may you sprinkle Amruta water of life and bring my child back to life :

Garuda (*Joyfully aside*)

The mention of Amruta has reminded me well. My ignorance is now washed off I believe. Now I shall go and implore Indra, the Lord of Heaven, and with the shower of Amruta given by him bring back to life not Jimutavahana alone but also these Nagas who had been eaten by me and whose bones alone are now left. And if he refuses to give it, then—

Tossing aside the ocean wlth the flap of my wings and stirring the wind into a gale with the speed of my flight,

Making the twelve suns and the submarine fire collapse helplessly before the blazing flash of my eyes,

Breaking into pieces Indra's bolt, Kubera's mace and Yama's club with my beak,

And then, dipping my wings in Amruta, I shall rain a shower of it in a moment.

Now, I am already off.

(*Exit*) **Jimutaketu**

Sankhachuda, why are you still waiting? Go, gather fuel and build up the pyre for my son, so that we too may be able to accompany him.

Old Queen

Sankhachuda, my child, do prepare it quickly, for your brother must be feeling uneasy without us.

Sankhachuda

As my elders command. But I shall certainly precede you in this matter.

(*Rising up and preparing the pyre*)

Old father, the pyre is ready.

Jimutaketu

Alas,—

> The excrescence on the head is still well marked, There is a lovely ring of hair between the brows.
> The eyes emulate a lotus and the chest vies with that of Vishnu (lion) while both the feet bear the sign of wheel.
>
> But ah, son ! why, by my sins, hast thou gone to eternal rest without attaining the status of a Vidyadhara Sovereign ?

Why weep, my Queen ? Get up, let us ascend the pyre.

(*All walk about*)

Malayavati (*with folded hands, looking upwards*)

O Goddess Gauri, thou hadst commanded that my husband would be a Vidyadhara Sovereign. Then how is it that in my case, accursed that I am, even thou hast proven thyself untrue ?

(*Enter Gauri in haste*)

Gauri

King Jimutaketu, don't, don't be so rash.

Jimutaketu

Oh ! here comes the Goddess Gauri, whose holy vision is never futile ?

Gauri (*Addressing Malayavati*)

Malayavati, my child, how have I proven myself untrue ? Look !

(*Approaching Jimutavahana and sprinkiling him with water from jug*)

I am pleased with you Jimutavahana, my son, who is the benefactor of all that lives

Even at the cost of your own life. Come thou back to life.

(*Jimutavahana sits up alive*)

Jimutaketu (*Joyfully*)

Congratulations, my Queen ! For, here is Jimutavahana resurrected unharmed.

Old Queen (*Joyfully*)

By the grace of the Goddess, he is.

(*Both fall at the feet of Gauri and then embrace Jimutavahana*)

Malayavati (*Cheerfully*)

My good luck, my lord has come to life again.

(*Falls at the feet of Gauri*)

Jimutavahana (*Seeing Gauri, folding his hands*)

O Goddess !—

O thou, who bestowes more than we ask for, who removes troubles of thy devotes,

Who are the sole refuge of all, Gauri, thou Goddess of Vidyadharas, I bow at thy feet.

(*Falls at her feet*)

Jimutaketu (*All look upwards*)

O, it's rain without clouds ! Goddess, what is thus ?

Gauri

King, it is the rain of Amruta, poured from Heaven by Garuda, the King of Birds, grown penitent, to bring back to life Jimutavahana and these skeletal remains of Nagas so far eaten by him.

(*Pointing by finger*)

Doesn,t the King behold—

These Nagas here, with their heads resplendent with lustrous hood-gems,

Rushing to enter the ocean with full speed like the swelling streams of Malaya hills,

By zig-zag paths leading to it, after having recovered their bodies intact,

licking the earth with the tips of their forked tongues through their avidity to taste the Water of Life ?

(*Addressing Jimutavahana*)

My child Jimutavahana, you deserve much more than merely the restoration to life, here I grant thee another boon.—

Now, of my own accord and pleasure, do I instantly make you the Emperor of Vidhyadharas

By anointing you with the most holy waters sprung from my own mind (Manasa) purer than those of the Manasa lake,

For they are free from the slimy sediment of the pollen of fallen lotuses

Shaken by the wings of swans, and are stored in jars of precious stone fashioned by my will.

Further,—

May this golden wheel, this white elephant with four tusks and also this sable steed as well as Malayavati

Be thy formost insignia. They are your real treasure, you have a good look at them.

And look ! here are all Vidyadhara chieftains, Matangadeva and others, offering tribute at my instance by bending their heads low in faithfulness, producing the bands of a rainbow with the flashing lustre of their crest-jewels. Tell me, my child, what other gift can I offer you ?

Jimutavahana (*Kneeling down*)

O, Bestower of favours ! What other gift greater than this could there be ?—

This Sankhachuda has been saved from the jaws of Garuda, and Vinata's son, has become humane,

The Nagas till now devoured by him have all been restored to life,

And, by my resurrection, my parents have been saved from putting an end to their life. I have obtained the sceptre of sovereignty from thee

We have been blessed by thy holy sight. What other boon, after all these favours, do still remain for me to ask ?

Nevertheless, let this much more be granted—

(*Epilogue*)

May the clouds send down timely rains stimulating the peacocks to dance mad with delight,

Making the earth wear a perennial garb of luxuriant green.

May tbe people, living righteously and free from scourge,

Assembling together with their friends and kinsmen in intimate picnics and parties, rejoice with their hearts free from rancour.

And also,—

May the worlds be all blessed with luck, may living beings devote themselves to doing good to others,

May calamities be stamped out, and may people he happy everywhere !

End of the fifth act finish (*Exeunt All*)